AF378377

THAI

Senior editor Wendy Bryant
Designer Caryl Wiggins
Contributing writer Karen Hammial
Food editor Louise Patniotis
Food director Pamela Clark
Special feature photographer Brett Stevens
Special feature stylist Trish Heagerty
Special feature food preparation Ariarne Bradshaw

ACP Books
Editorial director Susan Tomnay
Creative director Hieu Chi Nguyen
Director of sales Brian Cearnes
Marketing director Matt Dominello
Marketing manager Bridget Cody
Production manager Cedric Taylor
Chief executive officer John Alexander
Group publisher Pat Ingram
General manager Christine Whiston
Editorial director (WW) Deborah Thomas
WW food team Lyndey Milan, Alexandra Elliott,
Frances Abdallaoui

Cover Spicy sour prawn soup, page 36
Back cover Pumpkin, basil and chilli stir-fry, page 120
Photographer Brett Stevens
Stylist Trish Heagerty
Food preparation Ariarne Bradshaw

Photographers Alan Benson, Scott Cameron,
Ben Dearnley, Louise Lister, Brett Stevens,
Ian Wallace, John Paul Urizar
Pages 4, 5, 6, 10, 34, 46, 76, 104, 118,
152: Joe Filshie
Page 132: Getty Images

Stylists Wendy Berecry, Julz Beresford,
Marie-Helene Clauzon, Michaela le Compte,
Amber Keller, Sarah O'Brien, Louise Pickford

Produced by ACP books, Sydney, published by ACP Magazines Ltd.
54 Park St, Sydney NSW Australia 2000. GPO Box 4088, Sydney NSW 2001.
Ph: (02) 9282 8618 Fax: (02) 9267 9438.
www.acpbooks.com.au acpbooks@acpmagazines.com.au
To order books phone 136 116 (within Australia).
Send recipe enquiries to reccipeenquiries@acpmagazines.com.au
Printed by Tien Wah Press, 4 Pandan Crescent, Singapore, 128475

RIGHTS ENQUIRIES Laura Bamford, Director ACP Books. lbamford@acpmedia.co.uk

AUSTRALIA Distributed by Network Services,GPO Box 4088, Sydney, NSW 1028.
Ph: (02) 9282 8777 Fax: (02) 9264 3278.
networkweb@networkservicescompany.com.au
UNITED KINGDOM Distributed by Australian Consolidated Press (UK), Moulton Park
Business Centre, Red House Rd, Moulton Park, Northampton, NN3 6AQ
Ph: (01604) 497 531 Fax: (01604) 497 533 books@acpmedia.co.uk
CANADA Distributed by Whitecap Books Ltd, 351 Lynn Ave,
North Vancouver, BC, V7J 2C4 Ph: (604) 980 9852 Fax: (604) 980 8197
customerservice@whitecap.ca www.whitecap.ca
NEW ZEALAND Southern Publishers Group, 44 New North Rd,
Eden Terrace, Auckland.
Ph: (64 9) 309 6930 Fax: (64 9) 309 6170 hub@spg.co.nz
SOUTH AFRICA Distributed by PSD Promotions (Pty) Ltd, PO Box 1175,
Isando, 1600, Gauteng, Johannesburg, SA.
Ph: (011) 392 6065 Fax (011) 392 6079 orders@psdprom.co.za

Clark, Pamela.
The Australian Women's Weekly Thai
Includes index.
ISBN-13 978 1 86396 478 4
ISBN-10 1 86396 478 9
1. Cookery, Thai. I. Title.
I. Title. II Title: Australian Women's Weekly

641.59593
© ACP Magazines Ltd 2006
ABN 18 053 273 546

The publishers would like to thank the following for props used in photography:
Amerind Forest Products, Bodum, Ikea, littala, Design Mode International,
Major & Tom, Papaya, top 3 by design, Wheel & Barrow.

THE AUSTRALIAN
Women's Weekly

THAI

CONTENTS

one taste of Thai 6

menus 8

snacks & starters 10

soups 34

curries 46

stir-fries 76

seafood 104

vegetarian 118

rice & noodles 132

salads 152

curry pastes 174

glossary 176

index 182

conversion chart 184

One taste of Thai food and people become instant converts – it's the merging of flavours that does it – the freshness of vegetables and herbs with creamy coconut milk or pungent fish sauce. The seafood dishes, the salads, the noodles – it's the sort of food we like to eat today, light and fresh, but with a delicious twist that's entirely unique. And, nowadays, the fresh ingredients – limes, lemon grass, chillies and coriander – called for in much of this fabulous food are easy to buy. If the more unusual ingredients, such as fish sauce or pickled green peppercorns, are unavailable at your local supermarket, buy them at specialty Asian food stores as they will keep for ages. One of the world's great cuisines, the food of Thailand is neither difficult to make nor time-consuming, as you'll discover as you turn the page.

MENUS

dinner for friends

Sticky pork with kaffir lime leaves, page 27

Baked garlic quail, page 32

Chicken panang curry, page 67

Ginger beef stir-fry, page 98

Sweet soy fried noodles (pad sieu), page 141

Steamed jasmine rice, page 149

When feeding friends a Thai meal, serve it as they do in Bangkok: present all the food, with rice, at once, so everyone can take what they want when they want it.

barbecue

Barbecued chicken with chilli vinegar sauce, page 20

Mixed satay sticks, page 23

Salmon cutlets with green apple salad, page 113

Char-grilled beef salad, page 154

This selection is so filling, with sauces and salads in-built, so all you have to add is a large bowl of steamed jasmine rice and a tropical fruit platter.

banquet

Money bags, page 12

Fish cakes, page 28

Spicy sour prawn soup, page 36

Chicken green curry, page 48

Dry beef curry with onion and peanuts, page 75

Pork and lemon grass stir-fry, page 86

Vegetarian pad thai, page 124

Stir-fried eggplant tofu, page 127

Fried rice with prawns, page 137

Appetisers, soup, main courses, noodles and rice – this delectable assortment, served two or three at a time, progresses in a naturally complementary flow.

SNACKS & STARTERS

Thais love to snack. Wandering around the streets of Bangkok, you'll see and smell a wide variety of snacks and "fast food" eaten on the move. Thais also prefer not to eat a lot of one thing, but a little bit of a lot of different things throughout the day. In Thailand, these eating habits are easily satisfied by the wealth of tantalising "street food" sold along the pavements outside markets, shopping centres and business offices. And since their snacks often do double duty as openers to a main meal, you can make these recipes and eat them, any time, for any occasion, just like the Thais.

money bags

2 tablespoons peanut oil
1 clove garlic, crushed
1 small brown onion (80g),
    finely chopped
2cm piece fresh ginger (10g),
    chopped finely
80g beef mince
60g cooked small prawns,
    shelled, chopped finely
1 small carrot (70g), grated coarsely
2 green onions, chopped finely
1 tablespoon finely chopped
    fresh basil leaves
1 tablespoon white sugar

250g packet gow gee wrappers
1 egg, beaten lightly
vegetable oil, for deep-frying
sweet chilli sauce
½ cup (125ml) water
¼ cup (60ml) white vinegar
1 teaspoon hoisin sauce
1 fresh small red thai chilli,
    chopped finely
½ cup (110g) firmly packed
    brown sugar
1 fresh medium red chilli,
    sliced thinly

1 Heat peanut oil in medium frying pan; cook garlic, stirring, until lightly browned. Add brown onion and ginger; cook, stirring, 1 minute. Add beef; cook, stirring, until beef is browned through. Stir in prawn, carrot and green onion; cook 1 minute, cool. Stir in basil and sugar.
2 Make sweet chilli sauce.
3 Brush gow gee wrappers with egg, top with level teaspoons of beef mixture. Pull up edges of wrapper around mixture, pinch together to seal.
4 Heat vegetable oil in large saucepan; deep-fry money bags, in batches, until well browned, drain on absorbent paper. Serve hot money bags with hot sweet chilli sauce.

sweet chilli sauce Combine the water, vinegar, sauce, chopped chilli and sugar in small saucepan, stir over heat until sugar is dissolved. Bring to a boil; reduce heat, simmer, uncovered, about 5 minutes or until slightly thickened. Top with sliced chilli.

preparation time 35 minutes
cooking time 35 minutes
makes 30 money bags and ¾ cup sweet chilli sauce
per money bag 2.8g total fat (0.5g saturated fat); 205kJ (49 cal); 4.1g carbohydrate; 1.7g protein; 0.3g fibre
per tablespoon dipping sauce 0g total fat (0g saturated fat); 209kJ (50 cal); 12.1g carbohydrate; 0g protein; 0.1g fibre

spring rolls

20g rice vermicelli
2 teaspoons peanut oil
100g pork mince
1 clove garlic, crushed
1 fresh small red thai chilli,
 chopped finely
1 green onion, chopped finely
1 small carrot (70g), grated finely
1 teaspoon finely chopped coriander
 root and stem mixture
1 teaspoon fish sauce
50g cooked small prawns, shelled,
 chopped finely
1 teaspoon cornflour
2 teaspoons water
12 x 12cm-square spring roll wrappers
vegetable oil, for deep-frying

cucumber dipping sauce
1 lebanese cucumber, seeded,
 sliced thinly
½ cup (110g) white sugar
1 cup (250ml) water
½ cup (125ml) white vinegar
4cm piece fresh ginger (20g),
 grated finely
1 teaspoon salt
2 fresh small red thai chillies,
 sliced thinly
3 green onions, sliced thinly
1 tablespoon coarsely chopped
 fresh coriander

1 Place vermicelli in medium heatproof bowl; cover with boiling water. Stand until just tender; drain. Using kitchen scissors, cut vermicelli into random lengths.
2 Heat peanut oil in wok; stir-fry pork, garlic and chilli until pork is changed in colour. Add onion, carrot, coriander mixture, sauce and prawns; stir-fry until vegetables just soften. Place in small bowl with vermicelli; cool.
3 Blend cornflour with the water in another small bowl. Place 1 level tablespoon of the filling near one corner of each wrapper. Lightly brush edges of each wrapper with cornflour mixture; roll to enclose filling, folding in ends.
4 Make cucumber dipping sauce.
5 Just before serving, heat vegetable oil in wok; deep-fry spring rolls, in batches, until golden brown. Drain on absorbent paper; serve with cucumber dipping sauce.
cucumber dipping sauce Place cucumber in heatproof serving bowl. Combine sugar, the water, vinegar, ginger and salt in small saucepan, stir over heat without boiling until sugar is dissolved; pour over cucumber. Sprinkle with chilli, onion and coriander; refrigerate, covered, until cold.

preparation time
20 minutes
cooking time
20 minutes
(plus refrigeration time)
makes 12 spring rolls
and 1½ cups cucumber
dipping sauce
per spring roll 3g total fat
(0.6g saturated fat); 230kJ
(55 cal); 4g carbohydrate;
2.9g protein; 0.4g fibre
**per tablespoon dipping
sauce** 0g total fat
(0g saturated fat); 113kJ
(27 cal); 6.4g carbohydrate;
0.1g protein; 0.1g fibre

deep-fried stuffed chicken wings

12 large chicken wings (1.5kg)
500g chicken mince
2 green onions, chopped finely
2cm piece fresh ginger (10g),
    chopped finely
2 cloves garlic, crushed
1 fresh small red thai chilli,
    chopped finely
1 tablespoon cornflour
2 tablespoons cornflour, extra
1 egg, beaten lightly
1 cup (100g) packaged breadcrumbs
vegetable oil, for deep-frying

sweet chilli peanut sauce
½ cup (110g) white sugar
2 tablespoons water
2 tablespoons white vinegar
1 tablespoon coarsely chopped
    roasted unsalted peanuts
1 fresh small red thai chilli,
    chopped coarsely

1 Holding end of large third joint of wing, trim around bone with knife. Cut, scrape and push meat down to middle joint, without cutting skin. Twist bone; remove and discard bone. Repeat process with remaining wings.
2 Blend or process mince, onion, ginger, garlic, chilli and cornflour until combined. Using fingers, fill cavities of wings with mince mixture, secure ends with toothpicks.
3 Make sweet chilli peanut sauce.
4 Toss wings in extra cornflour, shake away excess. Dip into egg then breadcrumbs.
5 Heat oil in large saucepan, deep-fry wings until well browned and tender; drain on absorbent paper, remove toothpicks. Serve with sweet chilli peanut sauce.
sweet chilli peanut sauce Combine sugar and the water in small saucepan; stir over heat until sugar is dissolved. Bring to a boil; reduce heat, simmer, uncovered, 2 minutes, cool. Stir in vinegar, peanuts and chilli.

preparation time
50 minutes
cooking time
15 minutes
(plus cooling time)
makes 12 chicken wings
and ¾ cup sweet chilli
peanut sauce
per wing 19.2g total fat
(5g saturated fat); 1254kJ
(300 cal); 6.4g carbohydrate;
25.3g protein; 0.5g fibre
**per tablespoon dipping
sauce** 0.6g total fat
(0.1g saturated fat); 238kJ
(57 cal); 12.3g carbohydrate;
0.3g protein; 0.1g fibre

curry puffs

2 teaspoons peanut oil
2 teaspoons finely chopped
   coriander root
2 green onions, chopped finely
1 clove garlic, crushed
100g beef mince
½ teaspoon ground turmeric
½ teaspoon ground cumin
¼ teaspoon ground coriander
2 teaspoons fish sauce
1 tablespoon water
½ cup (110g) mashed potato

2 sheets ready-rolled frozen
   puff pastry
1 egg, beaten lightly
vegetable oil, for deep frying
sweet chilli dipping sauce
12 fresh small red thai chillies,
   chopped coarsely
8 cloves garlic, quartered
2 cups (500ml) white vinegar
1 cup (220g) caster sugar
2 teaspoons salt
2 teaspoons tamarind concentrate

1   Make sweet chilli dipping sauce.
2   Heat peanut oil in wok; stir-fry coriander root, onion, garlic and beef until beef is changed in colour. Add turmeric, cumin and ground coriander; stir-fry until fragrant. Add sauce and the water; simmer, uncovered, until mixture thickens. Stir in potato; cool.
3   Using 9cm cutter, cut four rounds from each pastry sheet. Place 1 level tablespoon of the filling in centre of each round; brush around edge lightly with egg. Fold pastry over to enclose filling, pressing edges together to seal.
4   Just before serving, heat vegetable oil in large saucepan; deep-fry curry puffs, in batches, until crisp and browned lightly. Drain on absorbent paper; serve with sweet chilli dipping sauce.
sweet chilli dipping sauce Place ingredients in medium saucepan, stir over heat without boiling until sugar is dissolved; bring to a boil. Reduce heat; simmer, uncovered, about 20 minutes or until slightly thickened. Cool 5 minutes; blend or process until smooth.

preparation time
30 minutes
cooking time
35 minutes
(plus cooling time)
makes 8 curry puffs and
1½ cups sweet chilli
dipping sauce
per curry puff 16.5g total fat
(2g saturated fat); 1016kJ
(243 cal); 17g carbohydrate;
6.3g protein; 1g fibre
**per tablespoon dipping
sauce** 0g total fat
(0g saturated fat); 217kJ
(52 cal); 12.5g carbohydrate;
0.1g protein; 0.3g fibre

barbecued chicken with chilli vinegar sauce

1kg chicken thigh fillets
2 tablespoons peanut oil
½ cup (125ml) coconut milk
paste
4 cloves garlic, crushed
1 teaspoon cracked
   black peppercorns
2 teaspoons white sugar
2 teaspoons ground turmeric
2 teaspoons hot paprika
1 tablespoon finely chopped
   fresh coriander root
1 teaspoon curry powder
2 fresh small red thai chillies,
   chopped finely
1 tablespoon peanut oil

chilli vinegar sauce
6 fresh small red thai chillies,
   chopped coarsely
4 cloves garlic, quartered
1 cup (250ml) white vinegar
½ cup (110g) caster sugar
1 teaspoon salt
1 teaspoon tamarind concentrate

1 Using mortar and pestle, crush ingredients for paste until mixture forms a paste.
2 Cut chicken in half, combine with paste and oil in large bowl; cover, refrigerate 3 hours or overnight.
3 Cook chicken on barbecue (or grill or grill plate) until browned and cooked through, basting frequently with coconut milk during cooking.
4 Meanwhile, make chilli vinegar sauce. Serve chicken with chilli vinegar sauce.
chilli vinegar sauce Place ingredients in medium saucepan, stir over heat, without boiling, until sugar is dissolved. Bring to a boil, reduce heat, simmer, uncovered, about 15 minutes or until slightly thickened; remove from heat, cool slightly. Blend or process until smooth.

Tamarind is one of the ingredients used in this sauce to add to the balance of flavours that readily identify it as Thai: sour, hot, sweet and salty. The tamarind concentrate adds a sour, tangy taste, the chillli, of course, gives it heat, while the sugar and salt proffer the obvious. Tamarind concentrate is used for ease: the tamarind pulp is distilled into a condensed, compacted paste, ready to use, with no soaking or straining required.

preparation time
20 minutes (plus refrigeration time)
cooking time
20 minutes
makes 10 chicken pieces and ¾ cup chilli vinegar sauce
per chicken piece
12.3g total fat (4.5g saturated fat); 840kJ (201 cal); 1.4g carbohydrate; 21g protein; 0.4g fibre
per tablespoon sauce 0g total fat (0g saturated fat); 217kJ (52 cal); 12.4g carbohydrate; 0.1g protein; 0.2g fibre

mixed satay sticks

250g chicken breast fillets
250g beef eye fillet
250g pork fillet
2 cloves garlic, crushed
2 teaspoons brown sugar
¼ teaspoon sambal oelek
1 teaspoon ground turmeric
¼ teaspoon curry powder
½ teaspoon ground cumin
½ teaspoon ground coriander
2 tablespoons peanut oil

satay sauce
½ cup (70g) roasted unsalted peanuts
2 tablespoons red curry paste
  (page 174)
¾ cup (180ml) coconut milk
¼ cup (60ml) chicken stock
1 tablespoon lime juice
1 tablespoon brown sugar

1 Cut chicken, beef and pork into long 1.5cm-thick strips; thread strips onto skewers. Place skewers, in single layer, on tray or in shallow baking dish; brush with combined garlic, sugar, sambal oelek, spices and oil. Cover; refrigerate 3 hours or overnight.

2 Make satay sauce.

3 Cook skewers on heated oiled grill plate (or grill or barbecue) until browned all over and cooked as desired. Serve immediately with satay sauce.

satay sauce Blend or process nuts until chopped finely; add paste, process until just combined. Bring coconut milk to a boil in small saucepan; add peanut mixture, whisking until smooth. Reduce heat, add stock; cook, stirring, about 3 minutes or until sauce thickens slightly. Add juice and sugar; cook, stirring, until sugar dissolves.

You need 12 bamboo skewers for this recipe. Soak the skewers in water for at least an hour before threading the meat onto them to help keep them from splintering or scorching. If a bamboo skewer does start to char, wrap a folded piece of foil around it to protect it.

preparation time 20 minutes
(plus refrigeration time)
cooking time 15 minutes
makes 12 skewers and 1¼ cups satay sauce
per skewer 6.8g total fat (1.9g saturated fat); 489kJ (117 cal); 0.6g carbohydrate; 13.2g protein; 0.1g fibre
per tablespoon satay sauce 5.7g total fat (2.6g saturated fat); 276kJ (66 cal); 2g carbohydrate; 1.6g protein; 0.9g fibre

deep-fried prawn balls

1kg cooked large prawns
5 green onions, chopped finely
2 cloves garlic, crushed
4 fresh small red thai chillies,
 chopped finely
1cm piece fresh ginger (5g),
 grated finely
1 tablespoon cornflour

2 teaspoons fish sauce
¼ cup coarsely chopped
 fresh coriander
¼ cup (25g) packaged breadcrumbs
½ cup (35g) stale breadcrumbs
vegetable oil, for deep-frying
⅓ cup (80ml) sweet chilli sauce

1 Shell and devein prawns; cut in half. Blend or process prawn halves, pulsing, until chopped coarsely. Place in large bowl with onion, garlic, chilli, ginger, cornflour, sauce and coriander; mix well.

2 Roll rounded tablespoons of prawn mixture into balls with wet hands. Roll prawn balls in combined breadcrumbs; place, in single layer, on plastic-wrap-lined tray. Cover; refrigerate 30 minutes.

3 Heat oil in wok; deep-fry prawn balls, in batches, until browned lightly and cooked through. Serve with sweet chilli sauce.

This version of seafood balls (also cooked as patties or cakes), made with prawns, is probably the one most preferred by westerners, but in Bangkok, where they're a classic appetiser, you'll also find them made of crab meat or white fish, filleted and minced. This is also a favourite snack of the Thais, and prawn balls are sold on the streets, just-cooked and slathered in hot chilli sauce, eaten by workers at lunchtime or by shoppers at any time.

preparation time
25 minutes
(plus refrigeration time)
cooking time
10 minutes
serves 4
per serving 10.9g total fat
(1.5g saturated fat); 1196kJ
(286 cal); 17.1g carbohydrate;
28.5g protein; 2.2g fibre

sticky pork with kaffir lime leaves

2 tablespoons peanut oil
300g minced pork
¾ cup (195g) grated palm sugar
⅓ cup (80ml) fish sauce
4 kaffir lime leaves, shredded thinly
½ cup (50g) deep-fried shallots
½ cup (50g) deep-fried garlic
½ cup (70g) coarsely chopped
   roasted unsalted peanuts
1½ cups lightly packed fresh
   coriander leaves

4 kaffir lime leaves, shredded
   thinly, extra
1 fresh long red chilli, sliced thinly
600g spinach, trimmed
1 lime (60g), cut into wedges
coriander paste
4 coriander roots
5 cloves garlic, chopped
12 white peppercorns

1   Heat half of the oil in large frying pan, add pork; cook, stirring, about 5 minutes or until browned lightly. Drain on absorbent paper; cool.

2   Meanwhile, make coriander paste.

3   Heat remaining oil in large frying pan, cook paste about 1 minute or until fragrant. Add sugar, sauce and lime leaves; simmer, uncovered, about 7 minutes or until mixture thickens.

4   Return pork to pan with half the shallots, half the garlic and half the peanuts; cook, uncovered, about 5 minutes or until mixture is sticky.

5   Add remaining shallots, garlic and peanuts to mixture. Stir in 1 cup of the coriander and extra lime leaves.

6   Top pork mixture with chilli and remaining coriander; serve with spinach leaves and lime wedges.

coriander paste Wash coriander roots thoroughly; chop coarsely. Using a mortar and pestle or food mill, crush the coriander roots, garlic and peppercorns to form a smooth paste.

Thais use all the coriander plant in their cooking to impart a stronger flavour to some dishes. This is why, when you buy a bunch of coriander at your local greengrocer, it is one of the very few fresh herbs that come with its stems and roots intact. Wash the leaves, stems and roots well before chopping them, and also scrape the roots with a small flat knife to remove some of the outer fibrous skin.

preparation time
20 minutes
cooking time
20 minutes
serves 8
per serving 12.8g total fat (2.5g saturated fat); 1175kJ (281 cal); 26.4g carbohydrate; 13.3g protein; 3.6g fibre

fish cakes

500g skinless redfish fillets, boned
2 tablespoons red curry paste
 (page 174)
2 fresh kaffir lime leaves, torn
2 green onions, chopped coarsely
1 tablespoon fish sauce
1 tablespoon lime juice

2 tablespoons finely chopped
 fresh coriander
3 snake beans (30g), chopped finely
2 fresh small red thai chillies,
 chopped finely
peanut oil, for deep-frying

1 Cut fish into small pieces. Blend or process fish with paste, lime leaves, onion, sauce and juice until mixture forms a smooth paste. Combine fish mixture in medium bowl with coriander, beans and chilli.
2 Roll heaped tablespoons of mixture into balls with wet hands; flatten balls into cake shape. Place on tray, cover, refrigerate at least 30 minutes.
3 Just before serving, heat oil in wok; deep-fry fish cakes, in batches, until browned lightly and cooked through. Drain on absorbent paper; serve with cucumber dipping sauce (page 15) and lime wedges, if desired.

There are a great many varieties of chilli used in Thai cooking – different ones are used for different dishes – but the most well-known must be "prik kee noo", a very short, small red capsicum variety we call a small red thai chilli, or "scud", which helps identify its héat quotient. About 3cm in length, it is one of the hottest members of the chilli family. Seed the chillies to lessen their intensity, but remember to wear disposable kitchen gloves when doing so.

preparation time
15 minutes
(plus refrigeration time)
cooking time 10 minutes
makes 16 fish cakes
per fish cake 3.7g total fat
(0.7g saturated fat); 263kJ
(63 cal); 0.4g carbohydrate;
6.7g protein; 0.4g fibre

crying tiger

50g dried tamarind
1 cup (250ml) boiling water
400g beef eye fillet
2 cloves garlic, crushed
2 teaspoons dried green
   peppercorns, crushed
1 tablespoon peanut oil
2 tablespoons fish sauce
2 tablespoons soy sauce
10cm stick (20g) fresh lemon grass,
   chopped finely
2 fresh small red thai chillies,
   chopped finely
1 large carrot (180g)
1 cup (80g) thinly sliced
   chinese cabbage

crying tiger sauce
¼ cup (60ml) fish sauce
¼ cup (60ml) lime juice
2 teaspoons grated palm sugar
1 teaspoon finely chopped dried
   red thai chilli
1 green onion, sliced thinly
2 teaspoons finely chopped
   fresh coriander
½ cup reserved tamarind pulp
   (see step 1)

1   Soak tamarind in the water for 30 minutes. Pour tamarind into a fine strainer set over a small bowl; push as much tamarind pulp through the strainer as possible, scraping underside of strainer occasionally. Discard any tamarind solids left in strainer; reserve ½ cup of pulp for the crying tiger sauce.
2   Halve beef lengthways. Combine remaining tamarind pulp, garlic, peppercorns, oil, sauces, lemon grass and chilli in large bowl; add beef, stir to coat beef all over in marinade. Cover; refrigerate 3 hours or overnight.
3   Make crying tiger sauce.
4   Cook beef on heated oiled grill plate (or grill or barbecue) about 10 minutes or until browned all over and cooked as desired. Cover beef; stand 10 minutes, slice thinly.
5   Meanwhile, cut carrot into 10cm lengths; slice each length thinly, cut slices into thin matchsticks.
6   Place sliced beef on serving dish with carrot and cabbage; serve crying tiger sauce separately.
crying tiger sauce   Combine ingredients in small bowl; whisk until sugar dissolves.

preparation time
20 minutes (plus standing
and refrigeration time)
cooking time
10 minutes
(plus standing time)
makes 4 servings of beef
and 1 cup crying tiger sauce
per serving 10.7g total fat
(3.3g saturated fat); 869kJ
(208 cal); 3.8g carbohydrate;
23.1g protein; 2g fibre
per tablespoon sauce
0g total fat
(0g saturated fat); 59kJ
(14 cal); 2.6g carbohydrate;
0.6g protein; 0.3g fibre

baked garlic quail

4 quails (640g)
4 cloves garlic, crushed
¼ cup (75g) sambal oelek
2 tablespoons honey

2 tablespoons light soy sauce
2 teaspoons brown sugar
2 tablespoons peanut oil

preparation time
15 minutes
(plus refrigeration time)
cooking time
25 minutes
makes 8
per half quail 9.1g total fat
(2g saturated fat); 510kJ
(122 cal); 2.1g carbohydrate;
7.9g protein; 0.5g fibre

1 Cut quails in half through centre of breast bones and either side of backbone; discard backbone.
2 Combine garlic, sambal oelek, honey, sauce, sugar and oil in medium bowl. Add quail; stir to coat quail all over in mixture. Cover; refrigerate overnight.
3 Preheat oven to moderate (180°C/160°C fan-forced).
4 Place quail on rack over baking dish; cook 15 minutes. Increase oven temperature to hot (220°C/200°C fan-forced); cook further 10 minutes or until quail are crisp and tender.

quail with fresh chilli and basil

4 quails (640g)
vegetable oil, for deep-frying
1 clove garlic, crushed
1 fresh small red thai chilli,
  chopped finely

1 tablespoon oyster sauce
1 tablespoon fish sauce
2 tablespoons shredded fresh
  basil leaves

preparation time
15 minutes
cooking time
15 minutes
serves 4
per serving 17.7g total fat
(3.4g saturated fat); 945kJ
(226 cal); 1.7g carbohydrate;
15.5g protein; 0.3g fibre

1 Cut quails in half through centre of breast bones and either side of backbone; discard backbone. Cut each quail half into three pieces.
2 Heat oil in wok; deep-fry quail pieces until browned and cooked through; drain on absorbent paper.
3 Leave 1 tablespoon oil in wok, discard remainder. Add garlic, chilli and sauces to wok; cook, stirring, 1 minute. Return quail to wok, stir until hot. Stir in basil.

โลๆ55
60
โลๆ:
45

SOUPS

A typical Thai meal, even breakfast, includes soup, served in individual bowls at the same time as the other, communal, dishes, with each diner mixing it, a spoonful at a time, with the rice on his plate. Tom yums are the most popular soups in Thailand. Tom translates loosely as broth or stock, while yum describes a spicy-sour tingling taste unchecked by the addition of mellowing coconut cream. Soup can also be eaten as a full meal when noodles or rice are added with various meats, seafood, tofu or vegetables; in Thailand, riverboat vendors and street stalls serve countless varieties of soup.

spicy sour prawn soup
tom yum goong

1.5 litres (6 cups) fish stock
1 tablespoon coarsely chopped
   coriander root and stem mixture
10cm stick (20g) fresh lemon grass,
   chopped finely
8 fresh kaffir lime leaves, torn
8cm piece fresh ginger (40g),
   sliced thinly
2 fresh small red thai chillies,
   sliced thinly

1 tablespoon fish sauce
12 uncooked large king
   prawns (840g)
8 green onions, cut into
   2cm lengths
⅓ cup (80ml) lime juice
⅔ cup loosely packed fresh
   coriander leaves
½ cup loosely packed fresh
   thai basil leaves, torn

1   Place stock, coriander root and stem mixture, lemon grass, lime leaves,
ginger, chilli and sauce in large saucepan, bring to a boil; reduce heat,
simmer, uncovered, 10 minutes.
2   Meanwhile, shell and devein prawns, leaving tails intact. Add prawns,
onion and juice to pan; simmer, uncovered, about 4 minutes or until prawns
just change in colour. Remove from heat; stir in coriander and basil leaves.

After removing the leaves, wash the stems and
roots of the coriander, scraping the root slightly
to remove the outer fibre. Chop them coarsely
then remove the tablespoon needed for this
recipe. Divide the remainder of the mixture into
tablespoon measures, and wrap each individually
in plastic and freeze to have on hand the next time
you want to make this most loved of Thai soups.
You'll need three juicy limes for this recipe.

preparation time
50 minutes
cooking time
15 minutes
(plus cooling time)
serves 4
per serving 1.6g total fat
(0.5g saturated fat); 606kJ
(145 cal); 4.5g carbohydrate;
27g protein; 1.2g fibre

spicy seafood soup

1 uncooked medium blue
   swimmer crab (325g)
200g firm white fish fillets
8 medium black mussels (200g)
150g squid hoods
1.25 litres (5 cups) chicken stock
2 x 10cm sticks (40g) fresh lemon grass,
   chopped finely
4cm piece fresh galangal (20g),
   sliced thinly
4 fresh kaffir lime leaves

6 small green thai chillies,
   chopped coarsely
4 dried long red thai chillies,
   chopped finely
8 uncooked large prawns (560g)
1 teaspoon grated palm sugar
2 tablespoons fish sauce
1 tablespoon lime juice
¼ cup loosely packed fresh
   thai basil leaves

1 Remove and discard back shell and gills of crab; rinse under cold water. Chop crab body into quarters, leaving claws intact. Cut fish into bite-sized portions; scrub mussels, remove beards. Score inside of squid hoods in a diagonal pattern; cut into 2cm slices.

2 Combine stock, lemon grass, galangal, lime leaves and the chillies in large saucepan; bring to a boil.

3 Add crab, fish, mussels, squid and unshelled prawns to boiling stock mixture; cook, uncovered, about 5 minutes or until seafood is just cooked through. Remove from heat (discard any mussels that do not open); stir in remaining ingredients. Serve hot.

The Thais sun-dry their chillies, but we can buy various types locally already dried: just be certain to buy sun- or oven-dried ones and not smoked, because the flavour is completely different. In Thai cooking, only the largest dried whole chillies are pulverised or ground for curry pastes or for addition to soups and stir-fries. They can be processed with or without the seeds, depending on how hot the dish is to be.

preparation time
20 minutes
cooking time
15 minutes
serves 4
per serving 3.7g total fat (1.3g saturated fat); 9.7kJ (217 cal); 5.9g carbohydrate; 39.2g protein; 0.9g fibre

mixed seafood soup

250g uncooked king prawns
6 baby octopus (540g)
2 litres (8 cups) water
2 tablespoons peanut oil
1 small brown onion (80g),
 chopped finely
3cm piece fresh ginger (15g), grated
3 cloves garlic, crushed
10cm stick (20g) fresh lemon grass,
 chopped finely
pinch saffron powder

1 fresh coriander root, chopped finely
1 teaspoon sweet chilli sauce
1½ tablespoons fish sauce
⅓ cup (80ml) lime juice
4 dried kaffir lime leaves
½ teaspoon cumin seeds
400ml coconut cream
1 tablespoon raw sugar
160g scallops
250g white fish fillets, chopped
2 tablespoons fresh coriander leaves

1   Shell prawns, reserve heads. Remove heads and beaks from octopus,
cut tentacles into pairs.
2   Combine reserved prawn heads with the water in large saucepan, bring
to a boil; reduce heat, simmer, uncovered, 30 minutes. Cool stock, strain into
large bowl; discard solids, reserve stock.
3   Heat oil in large saucepan, add onion, ginger, garlic, lemon grass, saffron,
coriander root and sauces; cook, stirring, until onion is soft.
4   Add reserved stock, juice, lime leaves and seeds, bring to a boil; reduce heat,
simmer, uncovered, 15 minutes. Stir in coconut cream and sugar, simmer 5 minutes.
5   Stir in seafood; simmer about 2 minutes or until seafood is cooked through.
Sprinkle with coriander leaves.

When you use fresh lemon grass, start
chopping from the white end, going
up only until you just reach the green
upper part of the stalk. Discard the
tough top green section. Lemon or
lime rind can be substituted for the
lemon grass in this recipe.

preparation time
25 minutes
cooking time
1 hour (plus cooling time)
serves 6
per serving 22g total fat
(13.6g saturated fat); 1576kJ
(377 cal); 7.1g carbohydrate;
37.1g protein; 1.8g fibre

chicken and galangal soup *tom kha gai*

3 cups (750ml) chicken stock
4cm piece fresh galangal (20g),
    sliced thickly
2 x 10cm sticks (40g) fresh lemon grass,
    cut into 5cm pieces
4 fresh kaffir lime leaves
2 teaspoons coarsely chopped
    coriander root and stem mixture
500g chicken thigh fillets, sliced thinly
200g drained canned straw
    mushrooms, rinsed
1 cup (250ml) coconut milk

1 tablespoon lime juice
1 tablespoon fish sauce
1 teaspoon grated palm sugar
¼ cup loosely packed fresh
    coriander leaves
2 fresh small red thai chillies,
    sliced thinly
2 fresh kaffir lime leaves,
    shredded, extra
10cm stick (20g) fresh lemon grass,
    sliced finely

1   Combine stock, galangal, lemon grass pieces, whole lime leaves and coriander
mixture in large saucepan, bring to a boil; reduce heat, simmer, covered, 5 minutes.
Remove from heat; stand 10 minutes. Strain stock through muslin into large
heatproof bowl; discard solids.
2   Return stock to same cleaned pan. Add chicken and mushrooms, bring to a boil;
reduce heat, simmer, uncovered, about 5 minutes or until chicken is cooked
through. Stir in coconut milk, juice, sauce and sugar; cook, stirring, until just
heated through (do not allow to boil).
3   Remove from heat; stir in coriander leaves, chilli, shredded lime leaves and
lemon grass slices.

Both the stems and roots of coriander are
used here, so be certain to buy a bunch of
fresh coriander with its roots intact. Wash
the coriander under cold water, removing
any dirt clinging to the roots.
Cut the two fresh lemon grass sticks into
5cm-long pieces, then, using the side of
a heavy knife, pound the pieces: bruising
them this way helps release the flavour into
the soup.

preparation time
15 minutes
cooking time
35 minutes
serves 4
per serving 19.2g total fat
(13.2g saturated fat); 1359kJ
(325 cal); 6.3g carbohydrate;
30.8g protein; 2.7g fibre

chicken and noodle soup

400g chicken breast fillets
2 cloves garlic, crushed
3 teaspoons ground cumin
½ teaspoon ground turmeric
1.5 litres (6 cups) chicken stock
1 tablespoon white sugar
½ teaspoon shrimp paste
3 teaspoons sambal oelek

2cm piece fresh galangal (10g),
　grated finely
50g rice vermicelli noodles
1 cup (80g) bean sprouts
3 lettuce leaves, shredded
2 tablespoons coarsely chopped
　fresh coriander

preparation time
15 minutes
cooking time
25 minutes
serves 6
per serving 4g total fat
(1.3g saturated fat); 577kJ
(138 cal); 7.4g carbohydrate;
17.6g protein; 1.2g fibre

1　Cut chicken into 2cm slices. Combine garlic, cumin and turmeric in large saucepan; stir over heat about 1 minute or until fragrant.
2　Add chicken, stock, sugar, paste, sambal oelek and galangal to pan; stir until combined. Bring to a boil; reduce heat, simmer, uncovered, 10 minutes.
3　Add vermicelli to pan; simmer 10 minutes.
4　Stir in bean sprouts, lettuce and coriander.

spicy beef soup

750ml (3 cups) water
750ml (3 cups) beef stock
6 green onions, chopped coarsely
2 cloves garlic, sliced
3 fresh coriander roots
2 tablespoons dark soy sauce
2 teaspoons brown sugar

1 fresh small red thai chilli,
　chopped finely
375g beef round steak, sliced thinly
425g can straw mushrooms, drained
¼ cup (60ml) lime juice
1 tablespoon coarsely chopped
　fresh coriander

preparation time
15 minutes
cooking time
25 minutes
serves 6
per serving 3.3g total fat
(1.4g saturated fat); 418kJ
(100 cal); 1.7g carbohydrate;
15g protein; 1.7g fibre

1　Combine the water stock, onion, garlic, coriander roots, sauce, sugar and half the chilli in large saucepan. Bring to a boil; reduce heat, simmer, uncovered, 15 minutes. Drain mixture. Return stock to same cleaned pan; discard solids.
2　Bring stock to a boil, add beef, mushrooms, remaining chilli and juice; reduce heat, simmer, uncovered, until beef is just cooked. Stir in coriander.

Soup can be prepared a
day ahead. Store, covered,
in refrigerator.

Soup can be prepared a
day ahead. Store, covered,
in refrigerator.

1/2
25

CURRIES

A major influence on Thai food has been the food introduced centuries ago by Indian traders travelling the Silk Road. The original Thai curries were a series of condiments added to the main meal of rice, but have evolved to become the many different robust dishes we eat today. While most Indian curries are made with ground dried spices, the defining ingredients of a Thai curry are fresh herbs, shrimp paste and fish sauce. Coconut milk, used in southern Indian food to disarm chilli heat, happily found a niche in the curries of the Thai kitchen.

chicken green curry

¼ cup (75g) green curry paste
  (page 174)
2 x 400ml cans coconut milk
2 fresh kaffir lime leaves, torn
2 tablespoons peanut oil
1kg chicken thigh fillets, trimmed,
  quartered
2 tablespoons fish sauce
2 tablespoons lime juice
1 tablespoon grated palm sugar

150g pea eggplants, quartered
1 small zucchini (90g), cut into
  5cm pieces
⅓ cup loosely packed fresh
  thai basil leaves
¼ cup coarsely chopped
  fresh coriander
1 tablespoon fresh coriander leaves
1 long green thai chilli, sliced thinly
2 green onions, sliced thinly

1 Place curry paste in large saucepan; stir over heat until fragrant.
Add coconut milk and lime leaves; bring to a boil, reduce heat.
Simmer, stirring, 5 minutes.
2 Meanwhile, heat oil in large frying pan; cook chicken, in batches,
until just browned. Drain on absorbent paper.
3 Add chicken, sauce, juice, sugar and eggplants to curry mixture;
simmer, covered, about 5 minutes or until eggplants are tender and
chicken is cooked through. Add zucchini, basil and chopped coriander;
cook, stirring, until zucchini is just tender.
4 Place curry in serving bowl; sprinkle with coriander leaves, sliced
chilli and onion.

You can substitute chicken breast fillets, but you'll
find that the thighs' more distinctive flavour stands
up to the robustness of the curry. Traditionally, the
chicken is not cooked separately first, as we have
done, but simply poached in the curry sauce. Not
only does this result in the curry having a higher fat
content, but the chicken fat can make the finished
dish look greasy or even curdled. Discarding the
fat left in the pan after browning the chicken will
have no effect on the flavour of the curry.

preparation time
20 minutes
cooking time
20 minutes
serves 4
per serving 67.1g total fat
(41.6g saturated fat); 3775kJ
(9.3 cal); 14.5g carbohydrate;
58.5g protein; 7.1g fibre

pork and pickled garlic green curry

Called a Northern Thai curry because it's a favourite of the residents of Chiang Mai, this curry is best made a day ahead so that the flavours can develop fully.

7cm piece fresh ginger (35g), chopped coarsely
3 cloves garlic, quartered
1 medium brown onion (150g), chopped coarsely
1 teaspoon ground turmeric
2 tablespoons green curry paste (page 174)
10 fresh kaffir lime leaves, torn

750g pork fillet, diced into 2cm cubes
¼ cup (60ml) peanut oil
1 tablespoon tamarind concentrate
1 cup (250ml) boiling water
2 tablespoons fish sauce
2 bulbs pickled garlic (50g), drained, chopped coarsely
2 teaspoons grated palm sugar

1   Blend or process ginger, fresh garlic, onion, turmeric, curry paste and half of the lime leaves until mixture is almost smooth; combine in large bowl with pork. Toss to coat pork all over in mixture; cover, refrigerate 30 minutes.
2   Heat oil in large saucepan; cook pork mixture, stirring, until browned lightly. Meanwhile, blend tamarind with the water in small jug; stir in sauce. Add tamarind mixture to pan; cook, uncovered, about 10 minutes or until pork is tender.
3   Add pickled garlic and sugar; simmer, stirring occasionally, about 5 minutes or until sauce thickens slightly.
4   Place curry in serving bowl; sprinkle with finely shredded remaining lime leaves.

Sweet and subtle pickled garlic, or kratiem dong, is the young green bulb, packed whole and unpeeled in vinegar brine. Eaten as a snack in Thailand, it can be served as a condiment to be sprinkled over noodle or rice dishes or can be used in cooking.

preparation time
20 minutes
(plus refrigeration time)
cooking time
20 minutes
serves 4
per serving 32.8g total fat (8g saturated fat); 2107kJ (504 cal); 7.8g carbohydrate; 42.7g protein; 4.6g fibre

pork curry with eggplant

750g pork fillets
¼ cup (60ml) coconut cream
2½ cups (625ml) coconut milk
1 medium eggplant (300g),
    chopped coarsely
1 tablespoon fish sauce
2cm piece fresh ginger (10g),
    grated finely
2 teaspoons grated palm sugar
3 small green thai chillies, sliced
3 fresh small red thai chillies, sliced
¼ cup firmly packed fresh basil leaves

curry paste
2 teaspoons dried chilli flakes
1 medium red onion (170g),
    chopped finely
3 cloves garlic, crushed
10cm stick (20g) fresh lemon grass,
    chopped finely
1 teaspoon galangal powder
2 teaspoons chopped fresh
    coriander root
1 teaspoon grated lime rind
½ teaspoon shrimp paste
1 dried kaffir lime leaf
1 teaspoon paprika
½ teaspoon ground turmeric
½ teaspoon cumin seeds
2 teaspoons peanut oil

1 Blend or process ingredients for curry paste until well blended.
2 Cut pork into 2cm slices, then cut slices in half. Combine coconut cream and curry paste in large saucepan; cook 1 minute or until fragrant. Add pork; cook 5 minutes.
3 Stir in coconut milk, eggplant, sauce, ginger, sugar and chillies. Bring to a boil; reduce heat, simmer, covered, until pork is tender. Stir in basil; serve with fresh lime wedges, if desired.

Thai eggplants come in a variety of different sizes and colours, but the closest in texture and taste to the one we use to make this dish, the plump egg-shaped dark purple one we all know, is a long, thin, purplish-green one found in shops specialising in South-East Asian produce. Yellow thai eggplant is not suitable: it is better used in chilli sauces.

preparation time
30 minutes
cooking time
20 minutes
serves 6
per serving 35.4g total fat (24.4g saturated fat); 1998kJ (478 cal); 8.7g carbohydrate; 30.2g protein; 3.9g fibre

pork jungle curry

2 tablespoons peanut oil
¼ cup (75g) red curry paste (page 174)
750g pork fillet, sliced thinly
⅓ cup firmly packed fresh thai
   basil leaves
40g pickled ka chai, sliced thinly
150g thai eggplants,
   chopped coarsely
1 medium carrot (120g), sliced thinly

100g snake beans, chopped coarsely
227g can bamboo shoots,
   rinsed, drained
2 x 5cm stems pickled green
   peppercorns (10g)
2 fresh kaffir lime leaves, torn
1 litre (4 cups) vegetable stock
4 fresh small red thai chillies,
   chopped coarsely

1 Place oil and curry paste in large saucepan; stir over heat until fragrant.
2 Add pork; cook, stirring, about 5 minutes or until browned all over.
3 Reserve about four large whole basil leaves for garnish. Add remaining basil leaves, ka chai, eggplant, carrot, beans, bamboo shoots, peppercorns, lime leaves and stock to pan. Bring to a boil, reduce heat; simmer, uncovered, about 10 minutes or until vegetables are tender. Stir in chilli.
4 Place curry in serving bowl; sprinkle with reserved basil leaves.

We used pickled thai green peppercorns, which are canned and still strung in clusters, but you can use an equivalent weight from a bottle of green peppercorns in brine. Without separating them from their strings, rinse and dry peppercorns before using.

preparation time
20 minutes
cooking time
20 minutes
serves 4
per serving 31.2g total fat (7.8g saturated fat); 2073kJ (496 cal); 6.5g carbohydrate; 45.3g protein; 5.1g fibre

seafood and thai eggplant yellow curry

500g squid hoods
400g firm white fish fillets
8 uncooked medium prawns (360g)
8 small black mussels (200g)
1 teaspoon shrimp paste
1 tablespoon peanut oil
2 tablespoons yellow curry paste
   (page 175)
2 cloves garlic, crushed
2cm piece fresh ginger (10g),
   grated finely
1 medium brown onion (150g),
   sliced thickly
10cm stick (20g) fresh lemon grass,
   chopped finely

1 fresh long red thai chilli,
   chopped coarsely
12 fresh thai eggplants (350g),
   quartered
1 cup (250ml) fish stock
400ml can coconut milk
3 fresh kaffir lime leaves, torn
1 tablespoon grated palm sugar
12 scallops (300g)
½ cup firmly packed fresh
   coriander leaves
2 tablespoons lime juice
2 fresh long red thai chillies,
   sliced thinly

1 Cut squid into 1.5cm slices. Cut fish into 3cm pieces. Shell and devein prawns, leaving tails intact. Scrub mussels; remove beards.

2 Wrap shrimp paste in foil, place in heated wok; roast, tossing, until fragrant. Discard foil, return shrimp paste to same heated pan with oil and curry paste; stir until combined.

3 Add garlic, ginger, onion, lemon grass and chopped chilli to wok; cook, stirring, until onion softens. Add eggplant; cook, stirring, 2 minutes. Add stock, coconut milk, lime leaves and sugar. Bring to a boil, reduce heat; simmer, stirring occasionally, 10 minutes.

4 Add fish; cook, uncovered, 3 minutes. Add remaining seafood; cook, covered, about 5 minutes or until prawns change colour and mussels open (discard any that do not). Stir in coriander and juice.

5 Place curry in serving bowls; sprinkle with sliced chilli and extra coriander leaves, if desired.

Fresh kaffir lime leaves are readily available in most greengrocers and many supermarkets. However, at a pinch, you can just as easily use fresh washed lemon or lime tree leaves or finely grated lime rind instead of the kaffir lime leaves (substitute each kaffir lime leaf with ½ teaspoon of finely grated lime rind).

preparation time
20 minutes
(plus refrigeration time)
cooking time
20 minutes
(plus cooling time)
serves 4
per serving 34.3g total fat (20.9g saturated fat); 2830kJ (677 cal); 14.2g carbohydrate; 74.9g protein; 6g fibre

fish and potato yellow curry

8 baby new potatoes (320g), halved
400ml can coconut milk
2 tablespoons yellow curry paste
   (page 175)
¼ cup (60ml) fish stock
2 tablespoons fish sauce
1 tablespoon lime juice
1 tablespoon grated palm sugar

800g firm white fish fillets, cut into
   3cm pieces
4 green onions, sliced thinly
⅓ cup coarsely chopped fresh
   coriander
1 fresh long red thai chilli, sliced thinly
1 tablespoon fresh coriander leaves

1 Boil, steam or microwave potato until almost tender; drain.
2 Meanwhile, place half of the coconut milk in large saucepan; bring to a boil. Boil, stirring, until reduced by half and the oil has separated from the coconut milk.
3 Add curry paste; cook, stirring, about 1 minute or until fragrant. Add remaining coconut milk, stock, sauce, juice and sugar; cook, stirring, until sugar dissolves.
4 Add fish and potato to pan; cook, stirring occasionally, about 3 minutes or until fish is cooked as desired.
5 Stir in onion and chopped coriander.
6 Place curry in serving bowl; sprinkle with chilli and coriander leaves.

Boiling half of the coconut milk down so that much of the watery content evaporates, makes the oil "separate" and come to the surface so you can "fry off" the curry paste in it rather than having to add any other oil.

preparation time
20 minutes
cooking time
20 minutes
serves 4
per serving 28.9g total fat (19.9g saturated fat); 2228kJ (533 cal); 19.5g carbohydrate; 46.6g protein; 5g fibre

fish ball and eggplant red curry

500g firm white fish fillets,
  chopped coarsely
1 clove garlic, quartered
1 tablespoon finely chopped
  coriander root and stem mixture
1 tablespoon soy sauce
1 tablespoon cornflour
2 teaspoons peanut oil
2 tablespoons red curry paste
  (page 174)
400ml can coconut milk

½ cup (60g) pea eggplants
2 teaspoons grated palm sugar
1 tablespoon lime juice
1 tablespoon fish sauce
2 green onions, sliced thinly
½ cup (40g) bean sprouts
2 fresh long red thai chillies,
  sliced thinly
¼ cup loosely packed fresh
  coriander leaves

1 Blend or process fish with garlic, coriander root and stem mixture, soy sauce and cornflour until mixture forms a smooth paste; roll heaped teaspoons of mixture into balls.

2 Place oil and curry paste in large saucepan; stir over heat until fragrant. Add coconut milk; bring to a boil, stirring, until combined. Add fish balls and eggplants, reduce heat; simmer, uncovered, about 5 minutes or until fish balls are cooked through. Add sugar, juice, fish sauce and onion; stir until sugar dissolves.

3 Place curry in serving bowl; sprinkle with sprouts, chilli and coriander leaves.

Tiny eggplants, about the size of peas (hence the English translation of their Thai name "makeua puang"), are usually found sold in clusters of 10 to 15 eggplants, similar to vine-ripened cherry tomatoes. While they are a bit more bitter than the larger round ones, this is one of the necessary flavours used as a foil to the richness of a rich, sweet coconut-sauced curry like this. They are sold fresh like grapes, or found pickled in jars; both can be found in Asian greengrocers and food shops.

preparation time
20 minutes
cooking time
15 minutes
serves 4
per serving 29.5g total fat
(19.8g saturated fat); 1789kJ
(428 cal); 10g carbohydrate;
29.5g protein; 4g fibre

duck red curry

¼ cup (75g) red curry paste (page 174)
400ml can coconut milk
½ cup (125ml) chicken stock
2 fresh kaffir lime leaves, torn
1 tablespoon fish sauce
1 tablespoon lime juice
⅓ cup firmly packed fresh thai
   basil leaves

1 whole barbecued duck (1kg),
   cut into 12 pieces
565g can lychees, rinsed, drained
225g can bamboo shoots,
   rinsed, drained
3 fresh long red thai chillies,
   sliced thinly

1 Place curry paste in large saucepan; stir over heat until fragrant. Add coconut milk, stock, lime leaves, sauce and juice. Bring to a boil, reduce heat; simmer, stirring, 5 minutes.
2 Reserve about eight small whole basil leaves for garnish; add remaining basil leaves, duck, lychees and bamboo shoots to curry mixture. Cook, stirring occasionally, about 5 minutes or until heated through.
3 Place curry in serving bowl; sprinkle with chilli and reserved basil leaves.

When you bring the curry paste mixture to a boil, don't cover the pan or the contents will boil over. Stirring constantly will assist with incorporating the curry paste into the coconut milk thoroughly, and helps prevent the mixture from "separating" (stops the oil in the coconut milk leaching out and forming a layer of greasy beads on the surface of the curry).

preparation time
15 minutes
cooking time
15 minutes
serves 4
per serving 63.9g total fat (29.9g saturated fat); 3377kJ (808 cal); 24.4g carbohydrate; 32.8g protein; 6g fibre

red chicken curry

2 tablespoons peanut oil
4 green onions, sliced thinly
750g chicken thigh fillets,
    chopped coarsely
2 tablespoons fish sauce
1 cup (250ml) coconut milk
1 red chilli, sliced thinly
curry paste
1 small red onion (100g),
    chopped finely
3 cloves garlic
10cm stick (20g) fresh lemon grass,
    chopped finely

3 teaspoons coarsely chopped
    fresh coriander root
2 teaspoons dried chilli flakes
1 teaspoon galangal powder
1 teaspoon grated lime rind
½ teaspoon shrimp paste
1 dried kaffir lime leaf
3 teaspoons hot paprika
½ teaspoon ground turmeric
½ teaspoon cumin seeds
3 teaspoons peanut oil

1   Blend or process ingredients for curry paste until smooth.
2   Heat oil in wok, add ⅓ cup of the curry paste and onion; cook, stirring,
about 2 minutes or until fragrant. (Reserve remaining curry paste for another use.)
3   Add chicken, in batches; stir-fry until just tender.
4   Return chicken to wok; stir in sauce and coconut milk. Bring to boil, reduce
heat; simmer, uncovered, until mixture is hot.
5   Top with sliced chilli.

Chilli flakes can be purchased almost everywhere
but it is easy to make your own and the guarantee of
freshness adds oomph to this recipe. Wash and coarsely
chop a handful of small red chillies. Dry roast them in a
preheated wok over moderate heat until they become
darker in colour and very aromatic. Take care that they
do not burn. Cool, then either blend or process them
into flakes, or crush using a mortar and pestle. Keep
them sealed tightly in a glass jar for up to three months.

preparation time
30 minutes
cooking time
15 minutes
serves 4
per serving 33.5g total fat
(15.9g saturated fat); 2048kJ
(490 cal); 5g carbohydrate;
41.6g protein; 2.2g fibre

chicken panang curry

2 x 400ml cans coconut milk
¼ cup panang curry paste (page 175)
2 tablespoons grated palm sugar
2 tablespoons fish sauce
2 fresh kaffir lime leaves, torn
2 tablespoons peanut oil
1kg chicken thigh fillets, quartered

100g snake beans, chopped coarsely
½ cup firmly packed fresh thai
  basil leaves
½ cup (70g) coarsely chopped
  roasted unsalted peanuts
2 fresh long red thai chillies,
  sliced thinly

1   Place coconut milk, paste, sugar, sauce and lime leaves in wok; bring to a boil, reduce heat. Simmer, stirring, about 15 minutes or until mixture reduces by about a third.
2   Meanwhile, heat oil in large frying pan; cook chicken, in batches, until browned lightly. Drain on absorbent paper.
3   Add beans, chicken and half of the basil leaves to curry mixture; cook, uncovered, stirring occasionally, about 5 minutes or until beans are just tender and chicken is cooked through.
4   Place curry in serving bowl; sprinkle with peanuts, chilli and remaining basil.
note Curry is best made just before serving. Paste can be made a week ahead. Store, covered, in the refrigerator.

Snake beans are long (about 40cm), thin, round, fresh green beans, Asian in origin, and have a taste similar to green or french beans. Used most frequently in stir-fries, they are also called yard-long beans because of their length.

preparation time
15 minutes
cooking time
20 minutes
serves 4
per serving 75g total fat (42.8g saturated fat); 4197kJ (1004 cal); 17.8g carbohydrate; 62.6g protein; 7.7g fibre

green curry vegetables

1 tablespoon peanut oil
1 medium brown onion (150g),
  sliced thinly
3 kaffir lime leaves, shredded finely
2 tablespoons green curry paste
  (page 174)
1 medium carrot (120g), sliced thinly
2 baby eggplants (120g), sliced thickly
3¼ cups (810ml) light coconut milk
100g button mushrooms, sliced thinly

4 medium yellow patty-pan squash
  (120g), quartered
100g snake beans, cut into
  5cm lengths
280g broccolini, chopped coarsely
1 small red capsicum (150g),
  sliced thinly
230g can sliced bamboo shoots,
  drained, rinsed
350g butternut pumpkin, sliced thinly

1 Heat oil in large saucepan, add onion and lime leaves; cook, stirring, until onion softens. Add paste; cook, stirring, until fragrant. Add carrot and eggplant; cook, uncovered, until eggplant is just tender.
2 Add coconut milk; bring to a boil, reduce heat. Add mushrooms and squash; simmer, uncovered, until squash is just tender. Add remaining ingredients; return to a boil. Reduce heat; simmer, stirring, about 5 minutes or until vegetables are tender.

Broccolini is milder and sweeter than traditional broccoli, is completely edible from flower to stem, and has a delicate flavour with a subtle, peppery edge. It is a cross between broccoli and chinese kale (also known as chinese broccoli or gai larn).

preparation time
20 minutes
cooking time
20 minutes
serves 4
per serving 51.1g total fat (38.2g saturated fat); 2587kJ (619 cal); 21.2g carbohydrate; 13.7g protein; 13.5g fibre

beef massaman curry

1kg beef skirt steak, cut into
   3cm pieces
1½ cups (375ml) beef stock
5 cardamom pods, bruised
¼ teaspoon ground clove
2 star anise
1 tablespoon grated palm sugar
2 tablespoons fish sauce
1 tablespoon tamarind concentrate
2 x 400ml cans coconut milk
2 tablespoons massaman curry paste
2 teaspoons tamarind concentrate,
   extra
½ cup (125ml) beef stock, extra
8 baby brown onions (200g), halved
1 medium kumara (400g),
   chopped coarsely
¼ cup (35g) coarsely chopped
   roasted unsalted peanuts
2 green onions, sliced thinly

massaman curry paste
20 dried long red chillies
1 teaspoon ground coriander
2 teaspoons ground cumin
2 teaspoons ground cinnamon
½ teaspoon ground cardamom
½ teaspoon ground clove
5 large cloves garlic, quartered
1 large brown onion (200g),
   chopped coarsely
2 x 10cm sticks (40g) fresh lemon grass,
   chopped finely
3 fresh kaffir lime leaves, sliced thinly
4cm piece fresh ginger (20g),
   chopped coarsely
2 teaspoons shrimp paste
1 tablespoon peanut oil

1 Place beef, stock, cardamom, clove, star anise, sugar, sauce, tamarind and half the coconut milk in large saucepan; bring to a boil, reduce heat. Simmer, uncovered, about 1 hour 30 minutes or until beef is almost tender.

2 Strain beef over large bowl; reserve spicy beef sauce, discard cardamom and star anise.

3 Place curry paste in same cleaned pan; stir over heat until fragrant. Add remaining coconut milk, extra tamarind and extra stock; bring to a boil, stirring, about 1 minute or until mixture is smooth. Add beef, brown onion, kumara and 1 cup of reserved spicy beef sauce; cook, uncovered, over medium heat, about 30 minutes or until vegetables and beef are tender.

4 Place curry in serving bowl; sprinkle with peanuts and green onion.

massaman curry paste Preheat oven to moderate (180°C/160°C fan-forced). Place whole chillies in small heatproof jug, cover with boiling water; stand 15 minutes, drain. Meanwhile, dry-fry ground spices in small frying pan over medium heat, stirring until fragrant. Place chillies and roasted spices in small shallow baking dish with remaining ingredients. Roast, uncovered, in moderate oven 15 minutes. Blend or process roasted curry paste mixture until smooth.

preparation time
35 minutes
cooking time
2 hours 20 minutes
serves 4
per serving 55.5g total fat (39.9g saturated fat); 3766kJ (901 cal); 29.6g carbohydrate; 67.7g protein; 7.9g fibre

beef curry with red and green chillies

2 cups (500ml) coconut milk
1kg beef rump steak, sliced thinly
¼ cup (60ml) coconut cream
2 teaspoons fish sauce
2 tablespoons raw sugar
4 green onions, chopped finely
2 tablespoons peanut oil
1 fresh small red thai chilli, sliced thinly
1 small green thai chilli, sliced thinly

curry paste
2 fresh small red thai chillies,
    chopped finely
3 cloves garlic, crushed
1 teaspoon finely chopped fresh
    lemon grass
1 teaspoon grated lime rind
1 teaspoon dried galangal
¼ teaspoon ground cardamom
2 green onions, chopped finely
½ teaspoon cracked black peppercorns
2 teaspoons finely chopped fresh
    coriander root
½ teaspoon shrimp paste
2 teaspoons lime juice

1 Using mortar and pestle, grind ingredients for curry paste to a paste.
2 Heat coconut milk in large saucepan; add beef, bring to a boil, reduce
heat. Simmer, uncovered, about 15 minutes or until beef is tender.
3 Heat coconut cream in separate saucepan; add curry paste, simmer,
uncovered, about 1 minute or until fragrant.
4 Stir paste mixture into beef mixture; bring to a boil, reduce heat. Simmer,
uncovered, until liquid is almost evaporated. Stir in sauce, sugar and onion.
5 Heat oil in small frying pan; cook chillies, stirring, about 2 minutes or until
crisp. Sprinkle chilli over curry just before serving.
note Curry is best made just before serving. Paste can be made a week ahead.
Store, covered, in the refrigerator.

Green chillies are always fresh chillies: they are the first
stage of ripeness of all chillies rather than a specific
variety. You can keep them frozen for months: buy a large
quantity when you find them, wash them thoroughly,
allow to air-dry then place in small amounts in snap-lock
plastic bags and freeze until you are ready to use them
Only thaw what you need each time and, for ease, slice
or chop them while they're still frozen.

preparation time
40 minutes
cooking time
25 minutes
serves 6
per serving 36.8g total fat
(23.1g saturated fat); 2220kJ
(531 cal); 9.9g carbohydrate;
39.8g protein; 2.2g fibre

dry beef curry with onions and peanuts

1kg beef chuck steak,
   chopped coarsely
3 cups (750ml) coconut milk
1 cup (140g) finely ground roasted
   unsalted peanuts
1 tablespoon fish sauce
2 teaspoons tamarind concentrate
6 baby onions (150g), quartered
¼ teaspoon ground cloves
¼ teaspoon ground cardamom
¼ teaspoon ground cinnamon
1½ tablespoons lime juice
1 teaspoon grated palm sugar

curry paste
2 teaspoons dried chilli flakes
1 medium red onion (170g),
   chopped finely
3 cloves garlic, crushed
10cm stick (20g) fresh lemon grass,
   chopped finely
1 teaspoon galangal powder
2 teaspoons finely chopped
   fresh coriander root
1 teaspoon grated lime rind
½ teaspoon shrimp paste
1 dried kaffir lime leaf
1 teaspoon paprika
½ teaspoon ground turmeric
½ teaspoon cumin seeds
2 teaspoons peanut oil

1   Blend or process ingredients for curry paste until well blended.
2   Combine beef, coconut milk and peanuts in large saucepan, bring
to a boil; reduce heat, simmer, covered, 1 hour, stirring occasionally.
3   Stir in curry paste, sauce, tamarind, onion, spices, juice and sugar;
simmer, uncovered, 10 minutes.
note   Recipe can be prepared a day ahead. Paste can be made a week
ahead. Store, covered, in the refrigerator. Recipe suitable to freeze.

This curry uses onions as an ingredient
as well as a flavouring. One of the most
important of all vegetables in Thai cooking,
small baby onions, shallots or pickling
onions are used in curry pastes, salads and
stir-fries, and for enhancing the aroma of
soups and stews. If they are small enough,
just peel the baby onions and add them
intact. Their slight resistance to the bite adds
crunch to a dry curry such as this one.

preparation time
30 minutes
cooking time
1 hour 15 minutes
serves 6
per serving 46g total fat
(27.8g saturated fat); 2642kJ
(632 cal); 10g carbohydrate;
43g protein; 5g fibre

STIR-FRIES

The original cooking methods native to Thailand were stewing and grilling, but the cuisine was greatly influenced by that of neighbouring China, home of stir-frying. This technique was embraced so emphatically that it now seems traditionally Thai and, to a degree, this is true. For a nation of people who snack round the clock, stir-frying food is as close to instant gratification as it gets. Plus, Thais have put a stamp on their stir-fries: almost every recipe includes chillies and garlic, and emanates a spicy pungency and herby freshness quite unlike that found in its Chinese ancestors.

chicken and thai basil stir-fry

2 tablespoons peanut oil
600g chicken breast fillets,
    sliced thinly
2 cloves garlic, crushed
1cm piece fresh ginger (5g),
    grated finely
4 fresh small red thai chillies,
    sliced thinly
4 fresh kaffir lime leaves, shredded
1 medium brown onion (150g),
    sliced thinly

100g mushrooms, quartered
1 large carrot (180g), sliced thinly
¼ cup (60ml) oyster sauce
1 tablespoon soy sauce
1 tablespoon fish sauce
⅓ cup (80ml) chicken stock
1 cup (80g) bean sprouts
¾ cup loosely packed fresh thai
    basil leaves

1   Heat half of the oil in wok; stir-fry chicken, in batches, until browned all over and cooked through.
2   Heat remaining oil in wok; stir-fry garlic, ginger, chilli, lime leaves and onion until onion softens and mixture is fragrant. Add mushrooms and carrot; stir-fry until carrot is just tender. Return chicken to wok with sauces and stock; stir-fry until sauce thickens slightly. Remove from heat; stir through sprouts and basil.

Stir-frying "in batches" results in the cooked chicken being removed from the wok before other ingredients are added. As well, cooking in batches means the pan is not overcrowed, which stops the meat from stewing.

preparation time
20 minutes
cooking time
15 minutes
serves 4
per serving 15.9g total fat (3.5g saturated fat); 1367kJ (327 cal); 9.2g carbohydrate; 35g protein; 3.4g fibre

tamarind duck stir-fry

25g dried tamarind
½ cup (125ml) boiling water
6cm piece fresh ginger (30g), peeled
1 tablespoon peanut oil
2 cloves garlic, crushed
2 fresh long red thai chillies,
    chopped finely
1 large whole barbecued duck (1kg),
    cut into 12 pieces
1 medium red capsicum (200g),
    sliced thinly

¼ cup (60ml) chicken stock
2 tablespoons oyster sauce
1 tablespoon fish sauce
2 tablespoons grated palm sugar
200g baby bok choy, chopped coarsely
100g snow peas, sliced thinly
8 green onions, cut into 5cm lengths
⅓ cup firmly packed fresh
    coriander leaves

1 Soak tamarind in the boiling water for 30 minutes. Pour tamarind into a fine strainer over a small bowl; push as much pulp through the strainer as possible, scraping underside of strainer occasionally. Discard any tamarind solids left in strainer; reserve pulp liquid.
2 Slice ginger thinly; stack slices, then slice again into thin slivers.
3 Heat oil in wok; stir-fry ginger, garlic and chilli until fragrant. Add duck and capsicum; stir-fry until capsicum is tender and duck is heated through.
4 Add stock, sauces, sugar and reserved pulp liquid, bring to a boil; boil, 1 minute. Reduce heat, add bok choy; stir-fry until just wilted. Add snow peas and onion; stir-fry until both are just tender. Remove from heat; stir through coriander.

Baby bok choy is sometimes called shanghai bok choy, chinese chard or white cabbage (pak kat farang); its mildly acrid, distinctively appealing taste has brought baby bok choy to the forefront of commonly used asian greens.

preparation time
20 minutes
(plus soaking time)
cooking time
10 minutes
serves 4
per serving 42.2g total fat (12g saturated fat); 2454kJ (587 cal); 19.3g carbohydrate; 32g protein; 3.4g fibre

stir-fried octopus with thai basil

1kg baby octopus
2 teaspoons peanut oil
2 teaspoons sesame oil
2 cloves garlic, crushed
2 fresh small red thai chillies,
  sliced thinly
2 large red capsicums (700g),
  sliced thinly

6 green onions, cut into 2cm lengths
¼ cup firmly packed fresh thai
  basil leaves
¼ cup (60ml) fish sauce
¼ cup (65g) grated palm sugar
1 tablespoon kecap manis

preparation time
20 minutes
cooking time
10 minutes
serves 4
per serving 6.7g total fat
(0.7g saturated fat); 1442kJ
(345 cal); 23.7g carbohydrate;
45.3g protein; 2.6g fibre

1 Remove and discard head and beak of each octopus; cut each octopus in half. Rinse under cold water; drain.
2 Heat peanut oil in wok; stir-fry octopus, in batches, until browned all over and tender. Cover to keep warm.
3 Heat sesame oil in wok; stir-fry garlic, chilli and capsicum until capsicum is just tender. Return octopus to wok with remaining ingredients; stir-fry until basil leaves wilt and sugar dissolves.

chicken, chilli and kaffir lime stir-fry

2 tablespoons vegetable oil
500g chicken thigh fillets, sliced thinly
2 fresh small red thai chillies,
  sliced thinly
2 cloves garlic, crushed
8cm piece fresh ginger (40g),
  grated finely
8 green onions, sliced thickly
½ cup (125ml) chicken stock
2 tablespoons lime juice

¼ cup (60ml) oyster sauce
2 tablespoons brown sugar
5 fresh kaffir lime leaves, shredded
500g fresh rice noodles
1 cup loosely packed thai basil leaves
250g bean sprouts
¼ cup (25g) fried shallots

preparation time
15 minutes
cooking time
10 minutes
serves 4
per serving 15.9g total fat
(2.8g saturated fat); 1843kJ
(441 cal); 40.2g carbohydrate;
32g protein; 3.8g fibre

1 Heat half of the oil in wok; stir-fry chicken, in batches, until browned lightly.
2 Heat remaining oil in wok; add chilli, garlic, ginger and onion; stir-fry until fragrant. Add stock, juice, sauce, sugar, lime leaves and noodles; bring to a boil.
3 Return chicken to wok with basil and sprouts; stir-fry until combined.
4 Serve sprinkled with fried shallots.

prawns with garlic *goong kratiem*

1kg uncooked medium prawns
2 teaspoons coarsely chopped fresh
   coriander root and stem mixture
2 teaspoons dried coriander seeds
1 teaspoon dried green peppercorns
4 cloves garlic, quartered
2 tablespoons peanut oil

1 cup (80g) bean sprouts
1 tablespoon finely chopped
   fresh coriander
1 tablespoon fried shallot
1 tablespoon fried garlic
1 tablespoon fresh coriander leaves

1 Shell and devein prawns, leaving tails intact.

2 Using mortar and pestle, crush coriander root and stem mixture, coriander seeds, peppercorns and garlic to a paste. Place paste in large bowl with prawns and half of the oil; toss to coat prawns in mixture. Cover; refrigerate 3 hours or overnight.

3 Heat remaining oil in wok; stir-fry prawn mixture, in batches, until prawns are changed in colour. Remove from heat; stir sprouts and chopped coriander through stir-fry. Serve sprinkled with fried shallot, fried garlic and coriander leaves.

Fried shallot (homm jiew) and fried garlic (kratiem jiew) are used as condiments on the table or sprinkled over cooked dishes. Both can be purchased canned or in cellophane bags at Asian grocery stores; once opened, leftovers will keep for months if tightly sealed. Make your own by slicing shallots or garlic thinly and shallow-frying in vegetable oil until golden-brown and crisp.

preparation time
20 minutes
(plus refrigeration time)
cooking time
5 minutes
serves 4
per serving 10.2g total fat
(1.8g saturated fat); 849kJ
(203 cal); 0.8g carbohydrate;
26.5g protein; 1.2g fibre

pork and lemon grass stir-fry

1 tablespoon peanut oil

10cm stick (20g) fresh lemon grass, chopped finely

2 fresh small red thai chillies, chopped finely

2 teaspoons finely grated fresh galangal

2 cloves garlic, crushed

500g pork mince

1 tablespoon red curry paste (page 174)

100g green beans, trimmed, chopped coarsely

2 tablespoons fish sauce

2 tablespoons lime juice

1 tablespoon grated palm sugar

1 small red onion (100g), sliced thinly

2 green onions, sliced thinly

¼ cup loosely packed fresh thai basil leaves

¼ cup firmly packed fresh coriander leaves

¼ cup (35g) roasted unsalted peanuts, chopped coarsely

4 large iceberg lettuce leaves

1 Heat oil in wok; stir-fry lemon grass, chilli, galangal and garlic until fragrant. Add pork; stir-fry about 5 minutes or until pork changes colour. Add paste; stir-fry until fragrant.

2 Add beans, sauce, juice and sugar to wok; stir-fry about 5 minutes or until beans are just tender. Remove from heat; stir in onions, herbs and half of the nuts.

3 Divide lettuce leaves among serving plates; spoon pork mixture into lettuce leaves, sprinkle with remaining nuts.

To remove the core from an iceberg lettuce, hold the core-end face down, then smash the lettuce down hard on the kitchen bench to loosen the outermost leaves so they'll come away without tearing. You can also hold the cored end of the lettuce under a strong burst from the cold water tap: the leaves will separate and fall into the sink intact.

preparation time
10 minutes
cooking time
15 minutes
serves 4
per serving 20.7g total fat (5g saturated fat); 1476kJ (353 cal); 8.3g carbohydrate; 31.5g protein; 3.9g fibre

Place the beef, wrapped tightly, in the freezer for an hour or so. This will firm it slightly and make slicing it very thinly much easier. Slice the meat against the grain.
Stir-frying meat "in batches" helps keep the oil as hot as possible so that all sides of the meat can be seared.

beef with oyster sauce

400g bok choy
250g chinese broccoli
2 tablespoons peanut oil
2 cloves garlic, crushed
500g beef rump steak, sliced thinly
50g snow peas

425g can baby corn, drained
6 green onions, chopped
2 tablespoons oyster sauce
1 tablespoon fish sauce
1 tablespoon brown sugar

preparation time
15 minutes
cooking time
10 minutes
serves 4
per serving 18.1g total fat
(5.4g saturated fat); 1463kJ
(350 cal); 10.6g carbohydrate;
33g protein; 6.7g fibre

1 Break bok choy and broccoli into large pieces; steam or microwave
until just tender, drain well. Cover to keep warm.
2 Heat oil in wok; stir-fry garlic and beef, in batches, until beef is browned
and just cooked.
3 Add peas, corn, onion, sauces and sugar to wok; stir-fry until peas are
almost tender.
4 Return beef to wok; stir-fry about 2 minutes or until heated through.
Serve mixture over bok choy and broccoli.

stir-fried steak with green beans

180g green beans
2 tablespoons peanut oil
1 medium brown onion (150g),
   chopped finely
2 cloves garlic, crushed
1 large green chilli, chopped finely

1 fresh large red chilli, chopped finely
500g beef rump steak, sliced thinly
1 tablespoon fish sauce
1 tablespoon finely chopped fresh
   coriander
1 teaspoon brown sugar

preparation time
15 minutes
cooking time
10 minutes
serves 4
per serving 17.7g total fat
(5.4g saturated fat); 1254kJ
(300 cal); 4.4g carbohydrate;
30.1g protein; 2.1g fibre

1 Slice beans diagonally. Heat half of the oil in wok; stir-fry onion, garlic, chillies
and beans until beans are just tender, remove from wok.
2 Heat remaining oil in wok; stir-fry beef, in batches, until browned and just cooked.
3 Return beef and bean mixture to wok with sauce, coriander and sugar; stir-fry
about 2 minutes or until mixture is heated through.

chilli beef with bamboo shoots

2 tablespoons peanut oil
1.2kg beef rump steak, sliced thinly
400g can bamboo shoots, drained,
   rinsed, sliced
2 fresh small red thai chillies,
   chopped finely
2 small green thai chillies,
   chopped finely
2 tablespoons fish sauce
1 dried kaffir lime leaf
1 teaspoon brown sugar
2 tablespoons chopped fresh basil

curry paste
5 dried red chillies
1 tablespoon chopped dried galangal
1 tablespoon chopped dried kaffir
   lime peel
1 cup (250g) water
2 green onions, chopped finely
2 cloves garlic, crushed
2 teaspoons grated lemon rind
10cm stick (20g) fresh lemon grass,
   chopped finely
1cm piece fresh ginger (5g),
   chopped finely

1 Make curry paste.
2 Heat oil in wok, stir-fry beef, in batches, until browned all over. Return beef to pan. Add ¼ cup curry paste, stir-fry 2 minutes.
3 Add bamboo shoots, chillies, sauce, lime leaf and sugar to wok; stir-fry until beef is tender. Stir in basil.
curry paste Combine chillies, galangal and peel in bowl, pour over the water; cover, stand several hours. Strain; reserve chilli mixture and ½ cup of the chilli liquid. Blend or process chilli mixture, reserved liquid, onion, garlic, rind, lemon grass and ginger until smooth.

Bamboo shoots, the pale yellow, edible first-growth of the plants, add crunch and fibre as well as a certain distinctive sweetness to a dish. In Thailand, bamboo shoots are available fresh during the rainy season (May to October), but the Thais, like us, buy them in cans and jars the rest of the year. There are many different types and sizes of bamboo shoots; the really big ones are usually sliced and used as an ingredient in a main course, while the smaller, finger-sized ones are eaten on their own, as a vegetable with sauce.

preparation time
30 minutes
(plus standing time)
cooking time
15 minutes
serves 8
per serving 14.7g total fat (5.3g saturated fat); 1158kJ (277 cal); 1.4g carbohydrate; 34.4g protein; 1g fibre

crisp hot and sweet beef with noodles

750g piece beef corned silverside
1kg fresh wide rice noodles
¼ cup (60ml) peanut oil
3 cloves garlic, crushed
3 fresh small red thai chillies,
   sliced thinly

4 spring onions, sliced thinly
2 tablespoons fish sauce
¼ cup (65g) grated palm sugar
1 cup firmly packed fresh
   coriander leaves

1   Place beef, in packaging, in large saucepan, cover with cold water; bring to a boil, uncovered. Reduce heat; simmer, covered, 1 hour 30 minutes. Remove from pan, discard packaging; drain beef on rack over tray for 15 minutes.
2   Meanwhile, place noodles in large heatproof bowl; cover with boiling water, separate with fork, drain.
3   Trim excess fat from beef. Using two forks, shred beef finely. Heat oil in wok; stir-fry beef, in batches, until browned all over and crisp. Drain on absorbent paper.
4   Stir-fry garlic, chilli and onion in wok until onion softens. Add sauce and sugar; stir-fry until sugar dissolves. Return beef to wok with noodles; stir-fry gently until heated through. Remove from heat; stir through coriander.

The fresh rice noodles used in this recipe can be found under various names – ho fun, sen yau, pho or kway tiau, depending on the nationality of the manufacturer. They can be purchased in various widths or, more commonly, in tea-towel-sized sheets weighing about 500g each that you can cut into the width you prefer.

preparation time
20 minutes
(plus standing time)
cooking time
1 hour 45 minutes
serves 4
per serving 23.8g total fat (6.4g saturated fat); 2905kJ (695 cal); 70.8g carbohydrate; 47.4g protein; 2.3g fibre

sticky pork on broccolini

1 tablespoon peanut oil
300g pork mince
2 cloves garlic, sliced thinly
½ cup (135g) grated palm sugar
2 tablespoons fish sauce
4 fresh kaffir lime leaves, shredded
½ cup (50g) fried shallots

½ cup (70g) chopped roasted peanuts
350g broccolini, halved crossways
1¼ cups loosely packed fresh
   coriander leaves
1 tablespoon lime juice
1 fresh long red chilli, sliced thinly

preparation time
15 minutes
cooking time
10 minutes
serves 4
per serving 19.9g total fat
(4.2g saturated fat); 1843kJ
(441 cal); 36.5g carbohydrate;
26g protein; 6g fibre

1   Heat oil in wok, add pork; stir-fry about 5 minutes or until browned lightly.
Add garlic; stir-fry about 1 minute. Drain on absorbent paper.
2   Add sugar, sauce and lime leaves to wok; bring to a boil; reduce heat, simmer,
uncovered, about 2 minutes or until thick. Return pork to wok with half of the
shallots and half of the peanuts; stir-fry about 2 minutes or until mixture is sticky,
but not too dry.
3   Meanwhile, boil, steam or microwave broccolini until just tender; drain well.
4   Stir 1 cup of the coriander into the pork mixture with the juice and remaining
shallots and peanuts.
5   Place broccolini on serving platter, top with pork mixture, remaining coriander
and chilli.

stir-fried sweet and sour vegetables

2 cloves garlic
2 fresh small red thai chillies
500g fresh asparagus
2 lebanese cucumbers (260g)
1 tablespoon peanut oil
100g snow peas

250g broccoli flowerets
1 medium green capsicum (200g),
   chopped coarsely
2 tablespoons fish sauce
1½ tablespoons white vinegar
1 tablespoon brown sugar

preparation time
20 minutes
cooking time
10 minutes
serves 6
per serving 3.4g total fat
(0.6g saturated fat); 368kJ
(88 cal); 6.3g carbohydrate;
5.8g protein; 4.4g fibre

1   Cut garlic and chillies into thin strips. Cut asparagus into 5cm lengths; cut
cucumbers in half lengthways, remove seeds, then slice thickly.
2   Heat oil in wok, stir-fry garlic and chillies until browned lightly; remove from
wok. Leave oil in wok.
3   Reheat oil in wok, add vegetables; stir-fry until vegetables are just tender.
4   Add combined sauce, vinegar and sugar; stir-fry 1 minute. Serve vegetables
sprinkled with garlic and chillies.

pork with eggplant

3 fresh small red thai chillies, halved
6 cloves garlic, quartered
1 medium brown onion (150g),
    chopped coarsely
500g baby eggplants
2 tablespoons peanut oil
500g pork mince
1 tablespoon fish sauce

1 tablespoon soy sauce
1 tablespoon grated palm sugar
4 purple thai shallots, sliced thinly
150g snake beans, cut into
    5cm lengths
1 cup loosely packed fresh thai
    basil leaves

1 Blend or process (or crush using mortar and pestle) chilli, garlic and onion until mixture forms a paste.
2 Quarter eggplants lengthways; slice each piece into 5cm lengths. Cook eggplant in large saucepan of boiling water until just tender; drain, pat dry with absorbent paper.
3 Heat oil in wok; stir-fry eggplant, in batches, until browned lightly. Drain on absorbent paper.
4 Stir-fry garlic paste in wok about 5 minutes or until browned lightly. Add pork; stir-fry until pork is changed in colour and cooked through. Add sauces and sugar; stir-fry until sugar dissolves. Add shallot and beans; stir-fry until beans are just tender.
5 Return eggplant to wok; stir-fry, tossing gently until combined. Remove from heat; stir through basil.

Purple thai shallots (homm) are also called asian or pink shallots; used throughout South-East Asia, they are a member of the onion family, but resemble garlic in that they grow in multiple-clove bulbs and are intensely flavoured. They are eaten fresh or deep-fried as a condiment, as well as used pounded in curry pastes or tossed through stir-fries.

preparation time
20 minutes
cooking time
25 minutes
serves 4
per serving 19.8g total fat
(5.1g saturated fat); 1484kJ
(355 cal); 10.7g carbohydrate;
31g protein; 5.7g fibre

ginger beef stir-fry

6cm piece fresh ginger (30g), peeled
2 tablespoons peanut oil
600g beef rump steak, sliced thinly
2 cloves garlic, crushed
120g snake beans, cut into
  5cm lengths
8 green onions, sliced thinly

2 teaspoons grated palm sugar
2 teaspoons oyster sauce
1 tablespoon fish sauce
1 tablespoon soy sauce
½ cup loosely packed fresh thai
  basil leaves

1 Slice ginger thinly; stack slices, then slice again into thin slivers.
2 Heat half of the oil in wok; stir-fry beef, in batches, until browned all over.
3 Heat remaining oil in wok; stir-fry ginger and garlic until fragrant. Add beans;
stir-fry until just tender.
4 Return beef to wok with onion, sugar and sauces; stir-fry until sugar dissolves
and beef is cooked as desired. Remove from heat; stir through basil.

Thai basil, or horapa, is different from holy basil and
sweet basil in both look and taste. Having smaller
leaves, it has a slight licorice or aniseed taste, and is
one of the basic flavours that typify Thai cuisine. The
leaves should be added to the wok off the heat, just
before serving this stir-fry.

preparation time
20 minutes
cooking time
10 minutes
serves 4
per serving 19.4g total fat
(6.2g saturated fat); 1421kJ
(340 cal); 4.6g carbohydrate;
35.9g protein; 1.9g fibre

stir-fried seafood with basil

200g white fish fillets
8 medium black mussels (200g)
250g uncooked large prawns
100g squid hoods
2 cloves garlic, crushed
1 fresh large red chilli, chopped finely
1 tablespoon coarsely chopped fresh
  coriander root

2 tablespoons peanut oil
100g scallops
2 tablespoons oyster sauce
2 tablespoons fish sauce
1 medium red capsicum (200g),
  sliced thinly
8 green onions, chopped
⅓ cup shredded fresh basil

1 Chop fish into 3cm pieces. Scrub mussels, remove beards. Shell and devein prawns, leaving tails intact. Cut squid into 6cm squares, score inside surface of squid using a sharp knife.
2 Using mortar and pestle, grind garlic, chilli and coriander to a paste. Heat oil in wok; cook paste, stirring, about 1 minute or until fragrant.
3 Add all seafood to wok; stir-fry until seafood is tender. (Discard any mussels that don't open.)
4 Stir in sauces, capsicum, onion and basil; stir-fry 2 minutes.

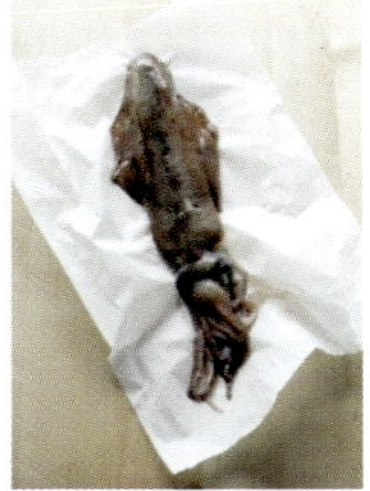

Squid is used in many of our favourite Thai dishes. It's made into a salad with unripe shredded mango, stuffed and served as a popular entrée, grilled and eaten with myriad herbs and chillies or, as here, stir-fried with other seafood, garlic and basil.

preparation time
30 minutes
cooking time
10 minutes
serves 4
per serving 11.4g total fat (2.3g saturated fat); 1003kJ (240 cal); 6.5g carbohydrate; 27.2g protein; 1.4g fibre

stir-fried vegetables with cracked black pepper

400g bok choy
2 tablespoons peanut oil
2 cloves garlic, crushed
3 medium carrots (360g), sliced thinly
250g beans, halved
1¼ cups (100g) bean sprouts

¼ cup (60ml) water
1 tablespoon fish sauce
1 tablespoon oyster sauce
1 teaspoon brown sugar
1 teaspoon cracked black
  peppercorns

preparation time
10 minutes
cooking time
10 minutes
serves 4
per serving 9.7g total fat
(1.7g saturated fat); 648kJ
(155 cal); 9.5g carbohydrate;
4.6g protein; 6.3g fibre

1 Break bok choy into large pieces. Heat oil in wok, stir-fry garlic, carrot and beans until vegetables are almost tender.
2 Stir in bok choy, sprouts, the water, sauces, sugar and peppercorns, bring to boil; reduce heat, simmer, uncovered, until vegetables are just tender.

lamb with basil and vegetables

2 cloves garlic
2 fresh large red chillies
1 medium carrot (120g)
1 medium brown onion (150g)
2 tablespoons peanut oil
1½ tablespoons tandoori curry paste

500g lamb fillets, sliced thinly
230g can bamboo shoots, drained,
  rinsed, sliced
4 green onions, chopped
⅓ cup shredded fresh basil
1 tablespoon fish sauce

preparation time
20 minutes
cooking time
15 minutes
serves 4
per serving 22.9g total fat
(6.9g saturated fat); 1450kJ
(347 cal); 5.5g carbohydrate;
28.3g protein; 3.5g fibre

1 Cut garlic, chillies and carrot into thin strips. Cut brown onion into wedges.
2 Heat half of the oil in wok, stir-fry garlic and chilli until browned lightly; remove from wok.
3 Reheat wok; stir-fry brown onion until soft, remove from wok.
4 Heat remaining oil in wok, add curry paste; stir-fry 1 minute. Add lamb; stir-fry lamb, in batches, until browned and just cooked.
5 Return lamb and onion to wok with carrots, bamboo shoots, green onion, basil and sauce; stir-fry until hot. Serve lamb mixture topped with garlic and chilli.
6 Serve with rice, if desired.

SEAFOOD

Not only does much of Thailand border long stretches of coastline, the heart of the region sits on a drainage basin crisscrossed by waterways that provide the country with an abundance of freshwater fish, crustaceans and molluscs. Seafood, regarded second only to rice in importance, has been a major food source for centuries. Fish sauce, shrimp paste, dried, salted and pickled fish and seafood provide essential flavours in almost every recipe, and are as inseparable from the taste of Thailand as coriander, chilli and lemon grass.

hot and sour fish steamed in banana leaves

4 medium whole bream (1kg)
1 large banana leaf
4 fresh small red thai chillies,
  sliced thinly
2 fresh kaffir lime leaves,
  shredded finely
2 green onions, sliced thinly
¼ cup loosely packed fresh
  coriander leaves
¼ cup loosely packed fresh
  thai basil leaves
2 x 10cm sticks (40g) fresh
  lemon grass
kitchen string

lime and sweet chilli dressing
¼ cup (60ml) sweet chilli sauce
2 tablespoons fish sauce
2 tablespoons lime juice
2 tablespoons peanut oil
1 clove garlic, crushed
1cm piece fresh ginger (5g),
  grated finely

1   Place ingredients for lime and sweet chilli dressing in screw-top jar;
shake well.
2   Score fish both sides through thickest part of flesh; place on large tray,
drizzle with half of the dressing. Cover; refrigerate 1 hour.
3   Meanwhile, trim banana leaf into four 30cm squares. Using tongs, dip one
square at a time into large saucepan of boiling water; remove immediately.
Rinse under cold water; pat dry with absorbent paper.
4   Place leaves on work surface. Combine chilli, lime leaves, onion, coriander
and basil in medium bowl. Halve lemon grass sticks lengthways, then halve
crossways; you will have eight pieces.
5   Place two pieces of lemon grass on each leaf; place one fish on each. Top
fish with equal amounts of the herb mixture. Fold opposite corners of the
leaf to enclose centre part of fish; secure each parcel with kitchen string.
6   Place two parcels, in single layer, in large bamboo steamer; steam, covered,
in two batches, over wok of simmering water about 15 minutes or until fish is
cooked through. Unwrap fish; drizzle with remaining dressing.

preparation time 10 minutes
(plus refrigeration time)
cooking time 20 minutes
serves 4
per serving 16.4 total fat (4.1g saturated fat); 1150kJ
(275 cal); 4.1g carbohydrate; 27.3g protein; 1.3g fibre

mixed seafood with crisp thai basil

250g squid hoods
250g firm white fish fillets
600g uncooked medium prawns
250g baby octopus
2 tablespoons peanut oil
1 clove garlic, crushed
2 fresh small red thai chillies,
  sliced thinly
1 medium carrot (120g), halved,
  sliced thinly

1 medium red capsicum (200g),
  sliced thinly
4 green onions, sliced thinly
1 tablespoon fish sauce
1 teaspoon oyster sauce
1 tablespoon lime juice
¼ cup (60ml) peanut oil, extra
⅓ cup loosely packed fresh thai
  basil leaves

1   Score squid in a diagonal pattern. Cut squid and fish into 3cm pieces; shell and devein prawns, leaving tails intact. Remove and discard head and beak of each octopus; cut each octopus in half. Rinse under cold water; drain.
2   Heat half of the oil in wok; stir-fry seafood, in batches, until prawns are changed in colour, fish is cooked as desired, and squid and octopus are tender. Cover to keep warm.
3   Heat remaining oil in wok; stir-fry garlic, chilli and carrot until carrot is just tender. Add capsicum; stir-fry until capsicum is just tender. Return seafood to wok with onion, sauces and juice; stir-fry until hot.
4   Heat extra peanut oil in small frying pan until sizzling; fry basil leaves, in batches, until crisp but still green. Drain on absorbent paper. Top seafood with basil leaves.

preparation time
25 minutes
cooking time
10 minutes
serves 4
per serving 26g total fat
(4.9g saturated fat); 1906kJ
(456 cal); 4.4g carbohydrate;
50.5g protein; 1.8g fibre

mussels with basil and lemon grass

1kg large mussels
1 tablespoon peanut oil
1 medium brown onion (150g),
   chopped finely
2 cloves garlic, crushed
10cm stick (20g) fresh lemon grass,
   chopped finely
1 fresh small red thai chilli,
   chopped finely

1 cup (250ml) dry white wine
2 tablespoons lime juice
2 tablespoons fish sauce
½ cup loosely packed fresh thai
   basil leaves
½ cup (125ml) coconut milk
1 fresh small red thai chilli, sliced thinly
2 green onions, sliced thinly

preparation time
20 minutes
cooking time
10 minutes
serves 4
per serving 12.1g total fat
(6.8g saturated fat); 886kJ
(212 cal); 6.9g carbohydrate;
8.4g protein; 1.7g fibre

1 Scrub mussels under cold water; remove beards.
2 Heat oil in wok; stir-fry brown onion, garlic, lemon grass and chopped chilli until onion softens and mixture is fragrant.
3 Add wine, juice and sauce; bring to a boil. Add mussels; reduce heat, simmer, covered, about 5 minutes or until mussels open (discard any that do not).
4 Meanwhile, shred half of the basil finely. Add shredded basil and coconut milk to wok; stir-fry until heated through. Place mussel mixture in serving bowl; sprinkle with sliced chilli, green onion and remaining basil.

fish in spicy coconut cream

2 teaspoons peanut oil
2 cloves garlic, crushed
1cm piece fresh ginger (5g),
   grated finely
20g piece fresh turmeric,
   grated finely
2 fresh small red thai chillies,
   sliced thinly

1½ cups (375ml) fish stock
400ml can coconut cream
20g piece fresh galangal, halved
10cm stick (20g) fresh lemon grass,
   cut into 2cm pieces
4 firm white fish fillets (800g)
2 tablespoons fish sauce
2 green onions, sliced thinly

preparation time
20 minutes
cooking time
30 minutes
serves 4
per serving 27.7g total fat
(0.8g saturated fat);
915kJ (219 cal);
26.3g carbohydrate;
15.3g protein; 11.2g fibre

1 Heat oil in wok; stir-fry garlic, ginger, turmeric and chilli until fragrant. Add stock, coconut cream, galangal and lemon grass; bring to a boil. Add fish, reduce heat; simmer, covered, about 8 minutes or until fish is cooked.
2 Using slotted spoon, remove fish carefully from sauce; place in serving bowl, cover to keep warm. Remove and discard galangal and lemon grass pieces from liquid. Bring liquid to a boil; boil 5 minutes. Remove from heat; stir in sauce and onion. Pour sauce over fish in bowl.

salmon cutlets with green apple salad

½ teaspoon sea salt
4 salmon cutlets (1kg)
2 medium apples (300g), sliced
   into matchsticks
2 green onions, sliced thinly
1 medium red onion (170g),
   sliced thinly
1½ cups loosely packed fresh
   mint leaves
¾ cup loosely packed fresh
   coriander leaves
½ cup (125ml) lemon juice
¾ cup (120g) roasted unsalted cashews

palm sugar dressing
⅓ cup (90g) grated palm sugar
2 tablespoons fish sauce
2cm piece fresh ginger (10g),
   grated finely

1   Make palm sugar dressing.
2   Sprinkle salt evenly over fish. Cook fish on heated oiled grill plate (or grill
or barbecue) until browned both sides and cooked as desired.
3   Meanwhile, combine apple, onions, mint, coriander and juice in large bowl;
pour over half of the palm sugar dressing, toss to combine.
4   Divide fish among serving plates; top with salad then cashews. Drizzle
remaining dressing over fish.
palm sugar dressing Combine ingredients in small saucepan; bring to a boil.
Remove from heat; strain. Cool before using.

In Thailand, this dish is made with jujubes (a fruit known as the "thai apple"), but we have substituted green apples for ease in obtaining ingredients. Called poodza in Thailand, the jujube is a small oval fruit, similar in taste and texture to an apple, which is eaten raw, juiced or dried. The fruit's thin edible skin changes from green to red as it ripens, which is when it is at its most sweet and crisp, like an apple.

preparation time
20 minutes
cooking time
15 minutes
serves 4
per serving 29.4g total fat
(5.8g saturated fat); 2583kJ
(618 cal); 38.3g carbohydrate;
46.9g protein; 5.4g fibre

baked fish with sweet and sour sauce

2 whole snapper (800g)
2 tablespoons fish sauce
1 tablespoon peanut oil
sweet and sour sauce
1 tablespoon peanut oil
2 cloves garlic, crushed
¼ teaspoon ground ginger
pinch chilli powder

2 tablespoons brown sugar
2 tablespoons white vinegar
2 tablespoons fish sauce
1 large tomato (220g), sliced thinly
1 small yellow capsicum (150g),
  chopped coarsely
4 baby carrots, sliced thinly
¼ cup (60ml) water

preparation time
15 minutes
cooking time
45 minutes
serves 4
per serving 11g total fat
(2.3g saturated fat); 1016kJ
(243 cal); 10.4g carbohydrate;
24.4g protein; 2.1g fibre

1 Preheat oven to moderate (180°C/160°C fan-forced).
2 Cut four deep slits into each side of fish, pour fish sauce into slits.
3 Heat oil in heavy baking dish; cook fish on both sides to seal, then bake,
covered, about 30 minutes or until cooked through.
4 Meanwhile make sweet and sour sauce.
5 Serve fish with hot sweet and sour sauce.
sweet and sour sauce Heat oil in large frying pan; cook garlic, ginger and
chilli, stirring, 1 minute. Add sugar, vinegar and sauce; stir over heat until sugar
is dissolved. Stir in remaining ingredients, bring to boil; simmer, covered,
about 3 minutes or until vegetables are just tender.

lemon grass and lime fish parcels

2 x 10cm sticks (40g) fresh lemon grass
½ cup coarsely chopped
  fresh coriander
1cm piece fresh ginger (5g),
  grated finely
3 cloves garlic, crushed
4 spring onions (100g), sliced thinly

2 fresh small red thai chillies,
  chopped finely
4 firm white fish fillets (800g)
1 lime, sliced thinly
1 tablespoon vegetable oil

preparation time
10 minutes
cooking time
20 minutes
serves 4
per serving 9.1g total fat
(2g saturated fat); 1078kJ
(258 cal); 1.5g carbohydrate;
41.5g protein; 1.2g fibre

1 Trim lemon grass; cut each piece in half lengthways.
2 Combine coriander, ginger, garlic, onion and chilli in small bowl.
3 Cut four sheets of foil, large enough to completely enclose fish. Place one
lemon grass piece on each foil sheet; top with fish then coriander mixture and
lime; drizzle with oil. Fold foil around fish to enclose completely.
4 Cook parcels on heated grill plate (or grill or barbecue) about 15 minutes
or until fish is cooked through.
5 Remove fish from foil before serving; discard lemon grass.

grilled fish with sweet-sour dressing

100g snow pea shoots, trimmed
1 cup loosely packed fresh mint leaves
½ cup loosely packed fresh
   coriander leaves
50g shallots, sliced thinly
2 fresh medium red chillies,
   sliced thinly

4 white fish fillets (800g)
⅓ cup (80ml) lime juice
2 tablespoons grated palm sugar
2 tablespoons fish sauce

preparation time
15 minutes
cooking time
10 minutes
serves 4
per serving 4.8g total fat
(1.5g saturated fat); 1200kJ
(287 cal); 14.2g carbohydrate;
44.8g protein; 2.6g fibre

1   Combine shoots, mint, coriander, shallot and chilli in medium bowl.
2   Cook fish on heated oiled grill plate (or grill or barbecue) about 4 minutes
or until browned both sides and cooked as desired.
3   Meanwhile, combine juice, sugar and sauce in small bowl.
4   Serve fish topped with salad and drizzled with lime dressing.

steamed fish with chilli and ginger

2 baby bok choy (300g), quartered
4 snapper cutlets (800g)
10cm piece fresh ginger (50g),
   cut into 4cm strips
2 green onions, cut into 4cm strips

¼ cup (60ml) salt-reduced soy sauce
1 teaspoon sesame oil
1 fresh large red chilli, sliced thinly
1 cup loosely packed fresh
   coriander leaves

preparation time
10 minutes
cooking time
10 minutes
serves 4
per serving 4.9g total fat
(1.3g saturated fat); 823kJ
(197 cal); 2.3g carbohydrate;
34.8g protein; 1.8g fibre

1   Place bok choy on large heatproof plate inside steamer; top with fish. Sprinkle
ginger and onion over fish, then spoon over sauce and oil. Cover steamer; steam
fish about 5 minutes or until just cooked through.
2   Serve fish topped with chilli and coriander.

VEGETARIAN

Being essentially a Buddhist country, Thailand is well acquainted with the concept of vegetarianism, so you're in luck when dining out on Thai food or cooking it at home. It is even simpler if you only avoid meat or poultry because so many of the flavouring ingredients are seafood-based. However, since a typical meal consists of many different dishes served at the same time, it's not hard to concentrate on the vegetable, tofu, rice, and noodle choices. And there's such a wealth of delectable tropical fruits and unusual vegetables in Thai cooking that you'll be spoiled for choice.

pumpkin, basil and chilli stir-fry

2 tablespoons peanut oil
1 large brown onion (200g),
   sliced thinly
2 cloves garlic, sliced thinly
4 fresh small red thai chillies,
   sliced thinly
1kg pumpkin, chopped coarsely
250g sugar snap peas

1 teaspoon grated palm sugar
¼ cup (60ml) vegetable stock
2 tablespoons soy sauce
¾ cup loosely packed opal
   basil leaves
4 green onions, sliced thinly
½ cup (70g) roasted unsalted
   peanuts, halved

1   Heat oil in wok; stir-fry brown onion, in batches, until browned and crisp. Drain on absorbent paper.
2   Stir-fry garlic and chilli in wok until fragrant. Add pumpkin; stir-fry until browned all over and just tender. Add peas, sugar, stock and sauce; stir-fry until sauce thickens slightly.
3   Remove from heat; toss basil, green onion and nuts through stir-fry until well combined. Serve topped with fried onion.

preparation time 10 minutes
cooking time 15 minutes
serves 4
per serving 18.5g total fat (3.5g saturated fat); 1321kJ (316 cal); 22.2g carbohydrate; 12.3g protein; 6.7g fibre

larb tofu

900g fresh firm silken tofu
peanut oil, for deep-frying
1 medium red onion (170g),
    chopped finely
½ cup coarsely chopped
    fresh coriander
10cm stick (20g) fresh lemon grass,
    chopped finely

2 fresh small red thai chillies,
    chopped finely
2 tablespoons lemon juice
1 teaspoon grated palm sugar
1 tablespoon soy sauce
½ teaspoon sambal oelek
8 small chinese cabbage leaves (360g)

1 Pat tofu with absorbent paper; chop finely. Spread tofu, in single layer, on absorbent-paper-lined tray; cover tofu with more absorbent paper, stand at least 20 minutes.

2 Heat oil in wok; deep-fry tofu, in batches, until browned lightly. Drain on absorbent paper.

3 Combine tofu in large bowl with onion, coriander, lemon grass and chilli. Combine juice, sugar, sauce and sambal oelek in small jug; stir until sugar dissolves. Pour dressing over tofu mixture; toss to combine. Serve larb spooned into individual cabbage leaves.

It is important the tofu is as well drained as possible before it is deep-fried. If you have time, a few hours before you want to make the larb, pat the whole piece of tofu with absorbent paper, then place it in a strainer or colander lined with absorbent paper set over a large bowl. Weight tofu with an upright saucer topped with a heavy can; allow to drain for up to 3 hours. Chop tofu just before deep-frying.

preparation time
20 minutes
(plus standing time)
cooking time
10 minutes
serves 4
per serving 27.6g total fat
(4.5g saturated fat); 1685kJ
(403 cal); 7.5g carbohydrate;
28.9g protein; 6g fibre

vegetarian pad thai

200g rice stick noodles
2 cloves garlic, quartered
2 tablespoons finely chopped
    preserved turnip
2 fresh small red thai chillies,
    chopped coarsely
¼ cup (60ml) peanut oil
2 eggs, beaten lightly
1 cup (90g) fried onion

125g fried tofu, cut into small pieces
¼ cup (35g) coarsely chopped roasted
    unsalted peanuts
3 cups (240g) bean sprouts
6 green onions, sliced thinly
2 tablespoons soy sauce
1 tablespoon lime juice
2 tablespoons coarsely chopped
    fresh coriander

1 Place noodles in large heatproof bowl; cover with boiling water, stand until noodles just soften, drain.

2 Meanwhile, using mortar and pestle, crush garlic, turnip and chilli until mixture forms a paste.

3 Heat 2 teaspoons of the oil in wok; pour in egg, swirl wok to make thin omelette. Cook, uncovered, until egg is just set. Remove from wok; roll omelette, cut into thin strips.

4 Heat remaining oil in wok; stir-fry garlic paste and fried onion until fragrant. Add tofu; stir-fry 1 minute. Add half of the nuts, half of the sprouts and half of the green onion; stir-fry until sprouts are just wilted. Add noodles, sauce and juice; stir-fry, tossing gently until combined. Remove from heat; toss omelette strips, coriander and remaining nuts, sprouts and green onion through pad thai.

Fried onion, sold in Asian grocery stores packed in jars or in cellophane bags, is used as a topping for Thai rice and noodle dishes, and is also served as a condiment as part of a Thai meal. Fried garlic is sold and used in the same way; both must be kept airtight to remain crisp. Soaking rice stick noodles (sen lek) in hot water before stir-frying makes them tender and helps prevent them from sticking together. Sen lek are the traditional noodles used in pad thai, and before soaking measure about 5mm in width; other thin rice noodles can be substituted.

preparation time
20 minutes
(plus standing time)
cooking time
10 minutes
serves 4
per serving 24.3g total fat
(4.4g saturated fat); 1417kJ
(339 cal); 15.2g carbohydrate;
13.4g protein; 4.3g fibre

stir-fried eggplant tofu

1 large eggplant (500g)
300g fresh firm silken tofu
1 medium brown onion (150g)
2 tablespoons peanut oil
1 clove garlic, crushed
2 fresh small red thai chillies,
  sliced thinly

1 tablespoon grated palm sugar
850g chinese broccoli,
  chopped coarsely
2 tablespoons lime juice
⅓ cup (80ml) soy sauce
⅓ cup coarsely chopped fresh
  thai basil

1 Cut unpeeled eggplant in half lengthways; cut each half into thin slices. Place eggplant in colander, sprinkle with salt; stand 30 minutes.
2 Meanwhile, pat tofu all over with absorbent paper; cut into 2cm pieces. Spread tofu, in single layer, on absorbent-paper-lined tray; cover tofu with more absorbent paper, stand at least 10 minutes.
3 Cut onion in half, then cut each half into thin even-size wedges. Rinse eggplant under cold water; pat dry with absorbent paper.
4 Heat oil in wok; stir-fry onion, garlic and chilli until onion softens. Add sugar; stir-fry until dissolved. Add eggplant; stir-fry, 1 minute. Add broccoli; stir-fry until just wilted. Add tofu, juice and sauce; stir-fry, tossing gently, until combined. Remove from heat; toss basil through stir-fry.

Chinese broccoli, also known as gai larn (kanah), gai lum or chinese kale, is appreciated more for its stems than its coarse leaves. It can be served steamed or stir-fried, in soups or in noodle dishes. Pour juice and sauce down the side of the wok rather than directly into the centre of the food, so that it is already sizzling by the time it touches the food and thus doesn't lower the temperature.

preparation time
15 minutes
(plus standing time)
cooking time
15 minutes
serves 4
per serving 15.3g total fat (2.4g saturated fat); 1241kJ (297 cal); 11.5g carbohydrate; 22.1g protein; 13.7g fibre

mixed vegetables in coconut milk

6 cloves garlic, quartered
3 fresh small red thai chillies,
    chopped coarsely
10cm stick (20g) fresh lemon grass,
    chopped finely
1 tablespoon coarsely chopped
    pickled galangal
4cm piece fresh ginger (20g),
    chopped coarsely
20g piece fresh turmeric,
    chopped coarsely
2 cups (500ml) coconut milk
2 fresh kaffir lime leaves

4 medium zucchini (480g),
    chopped coarsely
6 yellow patty-pan squash (240g),
    chopped coarsely
200g cauliflower florets
100g baby corn, halved lengthways
2 tablespoons soy sauce
2 tablespoons lime juice
⅓ cup coarsely chopped fresh
    thai basil
2 fresh kaffir lime leaves,
    shredded finely

1   Blend or process (or crush using mortar and pestle) garlic, chilli, lemon grass,
galangal, ginger and turmeric until mixture forms a paste.
2   Place half of the coconut milk in wok; bring to a boil. Add garlic paste; whisk
over high heat until smooth. Reduce heat, add remaining coconut milk and
whole lime leaves; simmer, stirring, until mixture thickens slightly.
3   Add zucchini, squash, cauliflower and corn; bring to a boil; reduce heat,
simmer, uncovered, about 5 minutes or until vegetables are just tender. Remove
from heat; remove and discard whole lime leaves. Stir sauce, juice and basil into
vegetable mixture; serve topped with shredded lime leaves.

Turmeric (kamin), a rhizome related to galangal and
ginger, must be grated or pounded to release its
somewhat acrid aroma and pungent flavour. Fresh
turmeric can be substituted with the more common
dried powder (use 2 teaspoons of ground turmeric plus
1 teaspoon of sugar for every 20g of fresh turmeric
called for in a recipe). Peel and cut any remaining fresh
turmeric and ginger into 20g pieces, then wrap
individually in plastic and freeze for future use. They'll
keep for months and are easier to grate when frozen.

preparation time
25 minutes
cooking time
15 minutes
serves 4
per serving 27g total fat
(22.8g saturated fat); 1467kJ
(351 cal); 15.1g carbohydrate;
8.6g protein; 8.6g fibre

stir-fried cauliflower, choy sum and snake beans

1 tablespoon peanut oil
2 cloves garlic, crushed
1 teaspoon ground turmeric
1 teaspoon finely chopped coriander
   root and stem mixture
4 green onions, sliced thinly
500g cauliflower florets

¼ cup (60ml) water
200g snake beans, cut into 5cm pieces
200g choy sum, chopped coarsely
1 tablespoon lime juice
1 tablespoon soy sauce
1 tablespoon coarsely chopped
   fresh coriander

preparation time
20 minutes
cooking time
10 minutes
serves 4
per serving 5.1g total fat
(0.8g saturated fat); 401kJ
(96 cal); 4.8g carbohydrate;
5.5g protein; 4.8g fibre

1 Heat oil in wok; stir-fry garlic, turmeric, coriander root and stem mixture and onion until onion just softens. Remove from wok; cover to keep warm.
2 Stir-fry cauliflower with the water in wok until cauliflower is almost tender. Add beans and choy sum; stir-fry until vegetables are just tender.
3 Add juice, sauce, chopped coriander and onion mixture; stir-fry until heated through.

deep-fried tofu with peanut sauce

900g fresh firm silken tofu
peanut oil, for deep-frying
peanut sauce
1 fresh coriander root, chopped finely
1 fresh small red thai chilli,
   chopped finely

2 cloves garlic, crushed
1 tablespoon brown sugar
2 tablespoons rice vinegar
⅓ cup (95g) smooth peanut butter
¼ cup (60ml) coconut milk

preparation time
20 minutes
(plus standing time)
cooking time
20 minutes
serves 6
per serving 28.6g total fat
(6.2g saturated fat); 1576kJ
(377 cal); 6g carbohydrate;
22.4g protein; 4.8g fibre

1 Pat tofu with absorbent paper; cut into 2cm pieces. Spread tofu, in single layer, on absorbent-paper-lined tray; cover with more paper, stand at least 20 minutes.
2 Make peanut sauce.
3 Heat oil in wok; deep-fry tofu, in batches, until well browned; drain. Serve hot tofu with warm peanut sauce; sprinkle with fresh coriander and chilli, if desired.
peanut sauce Combine coriander, chilli, garlic, sugar and vinegar in small saucepan, stir over heat until sugar dissolves. Add peanut butter and coconut milk; stir until hot.

RICE & NOODLES

Rice is so important to the well-being of the Thais that the literal translation of a common greeting is, "Have you eaten rice yet today?". With its very own goddess, the grain has achieved supreme importance: not only is it the mainstay of the Thai diet, but of the economy, too – Thailand being the world's largest exporter of rice. Most of the noodles in Thailand are made from rice flour, and a dish of crisp mee krob at one of Bangkok's myriad noodle stalls is a culinary delight. In fact, the quest for the perfect bowl of noodles has become an obsession for many Thai foodlovers.

thai fried rice stick noodles
pad thai

40g tamarind pulp
½ cup (125ml) boiling water
2 tablespoons grated palm sugar
⅓ cup (80ml) sweet chilli sauce
⅓ cup (80ml) fish sauce
375g rice stick noodles
12 uncooked medium prawns (540g)
2 cloves garlic, crushed
2 tablespoons finely chopped
  preserved turnip
2 tablespoons dried shrimp
4cm piece fresh ginger (20g),
  grated finely

2 fresh small red thai chillies,
  chopped coarsely
1 tablespoon peanut oil
250g pork mince
3 eggs, beaten lightly
2 cups (160g) bean sprouts
4 green onions, sliced thinly
⅓ cup coarsely chopped
  fresh coriander
¼ cup (35g) coarsely chopped
  roasted unsalted peanuts
1 lime, quartered

1   Soak tamarind pulp in the boiling water for 30 minutes. Pour tamarind into fine strainer over small bowl; push as much tamarind pulp through strainer as possible, scraping underside of strainer occasionally. Discard any tamarind solids left in strainer; reserve pulp liquid in bowl. Mix sugar and sauces into bowl with pulp liquid.
2   Meanwhile, place noodles in large heatproof bowl; cover with boiling water, stand until noodles just soften; drain.
3   Shell and devein prawns, leaving tails intact.
4   Blend or process (or crush using mortar and pestle) garlic, turnip, shrimp, ginger and chilli until mixture forms a paste.
5   Heat oil in wok; stir-fry paste until fragrant. Add pork; stir-fry until just cooked through. Add prawns; stir-fry 1 minute. Add egg; stir-fry until egg just sets. Add noodles, tamarind mixture, sprouts and half of the onion; stir-fry, tossing gently until combined. Remove from heat; add remaining green onion, coriander and nuts, toss gently until combined. Serve with lime wedges.

preparation time 20 minutes (plus standing time)
cooking time 10 minutes
serves 4
per serving 19.7g total fat (4.5g saturated fat); 2608kJ (624 cal); 65.6g carbohydrate; 42.6g protein; 5.4g fibre

fried rice with prawns

1 cup (200g) long-grain rice
10g dried shiitake mushrooms
400g can baby corn, drained
500g cooked king prawns, shelled
¼ cup (60ml) peanut oil
3 eggs, beaten lightly
1 medium brown onion (150g),
  chopped finely
2 cloves garlic, crushed
1 pork butterfly steak (160g),
  chopped finely

2 seafood sticks (65g), sliced thinly
1 medium green capsicum (200g),
  chopped finely
1 tablespoon red curry paste (page 174)
2 tablespoons light soy sauce
1 tablespoon fish sauce
1 tablespoon finely chopped
  fresh coriander

1 Rinse rice under cold water, drain. Add rice to large saucepan of boiling water. Boil, uncovered, about 10 minutes or until tender. Drain, rinse rice under cold water, drain.
2 Place mushrooms in bowl, cover with warm water, stand 20 minutes. Drain mushrooms, discard stems, cut caps into thin slices. Cut corn into quarters. Cut prawns in half lengthways.
3 Heat 1 tablespoon of the oil in wok, add egg; swirl wok to make thin omelette. Remove omelette from wok, roll up firmly, cut into thin slices.
4 Heat remaining oil in wok, stir-fry onion and garlic 30 seconds. Add pork, stir-fry until browned. Add prawns, seafood sticks, capsicum and paste; stir-fry 2 minutes. Add rice, sauces and coriander; stir-fry until hot. Serve rice topped with omelette slices.

Seafood sticks, a frozen ready-to-eat fish mixture, are used throughout Asia as a substitute for more expensive seafood, particularly crab and lobster. We used it in this recipe instead of the more typical ingredient found in most fried rice variations, dried chinese sausage. Seafood sticks, a popular ingredient in sushi, are available from Asian grocers and some fishmongers.

preparation time
30 minutes
(plus standing time)
cooking time
30 minutes
serves 6
per serving 15.5g total fat (3.3g saturated fat); 1530kJ (366 cal); 31.3g carbohydrate; 23.6g protein; 3g fibre

chicken and thai basil fried rice

¼ cup (60ml) peanut oil
1 medium brown onion (150g),
    chopped finely
3 cloves garlic, crushed
2 long green thai chillies,
    chopped finely
1 tablespoon brown sugar
500g chicken breast fillets,
    chopped coarsely

2 medium red capsicums (400g),
    sliced thinly
200g green beans, chopped coarsely
4 cups cooked jasmine rice
2 tablespoons fish sauce
2 tablespoons soy sauce
½ cup loosely packed fresh thai
    basil leaves

1 Heat oil in wok; stir-fry onion, garlic and chilli until onion softens. Add sugar; stir-fry until dissolved. Add chicken; stir-fry until browned lightly. Add capsicum and beans; stir-fry until vegetables are just tender and chicken is cooked through.
2 Add rice and sauces; stir-fry, tossing gently until combined. Remove from heat; add basil, toss gently to combine.

One of the secrets to making perfect fried rice is that the rice must be cold before using it. Make the rice far enough in advance so that it is chilled completely and quite dry, in order to prevent it sticking together in clumps when added to the wok. After cooking the rice, drain it if necessary, then spread in a single layer on a tray lined with baking paper or greaseproof paper. Cover with absorbent paper (condensation trapped below plastic wrap will keep the rice too wet) and refrigerate for at least 3 hours or overnight.

preparation time
15 minutes
cooking time
10 minutes
serves 4
per serving 19.7g total fat (4g saturated fat); 2445kJ (585 cal); 64g carbohydrate; 34.8g protein; 5g fibre

sweet soy fried noodles *pad sieu*

1kg fresh wide rice noodles
2 teaspoons sesame oil
2 cloves garlic, crushed
2 fresh small red thai chillies,
  sliced thinly
600g chicken thigh fillets,
  chopped coarsely
250g baby bok choy,
  quartered lengthways

4 green onions, sliced thinly
2 tablespoons kecap manis
1 tablespoon oyster sauce
1 tablespoon fish sauce
1 tablespoon grated palm sugar
¼ cup coarsely chopped fresh
  coriander
1 tablespoon fried onion

1 Place noodles in large heatproof bowl; cover with boiling water, separate noodles with fork, drain.

2 Heat oil in large wok; stir-fry garlic and chilli until fragrant. Add chicken; stir-fry until browned lightly. Add bok choy and green onion; stir-fry until onion softens and chicken is cooked through.

3 Add noodles, kecap manis, sauces and sugar to wok; stir-fry, tossing gently to combine. Remove from heat; add coriander, toss gently to combine. Sprinkle with fried onion.

The fresh rice noodles used in this recipe can be found under various names – ho fun, sen yau, pho or kway tiau, depending on the nationality of the manufacturer. They can be purchased in various widths or sheets weighing about 500g each, which you cut into the noodle width you prefer. These noodles do not need pre-cooking, but do require a hot-water "bath" in order to separate them into individual strands.

preparation time
15 minutes
cooking time
15 minutes
serves 4
per serving 10g total fat (2.2g saturated fat); 2057kJ (492 cal); 59.9g carbohydrate; 38.3g protein; 2.7g fibre

crisp fried noodles *mee krob*

150g fresh firm silken tofu
vegetable oil, for deep-frying
125g rice vermicelli noodles
2 tablespoons peanut oil
2 eggs, beaten lightly
1 tablespoon water
2 cloves garlic, crushed
2 fresh small red thai chillies,
   chopped finely
1 small green thai chilli,
   chopped finely

2 tablespoons grated palm sugar
2 tablespoons fish sauce
2 tablespoons tomato sauce
1 tablespoon rice wine vinegar
200g pork mince
200g cooked small prawns, shelled,
   chopped coarsely
6 green onions, sliced thinly
¼ cup firmly packed fresh
   coriander leaves

1   Pat tofu all over with absorbent paper; cut into slices, then cut each slice into
1cm-wide matchsticks. Spread tofu, in single layer, on absorbent-paper-lined tray;
cover tofu with more absorbent paper, stand at least 20 minutes.
2   Meanwhile, heat vegetable oil in wok; deep-fry vermicelli quickly, in batches,
until puffed. Drain on absorbent paper.
3   Using same heated oil, deep-fry drained tofu, in batches, until browned lightly.
Drain on absorbent paper. Discard oil from wok.
4   Heat 2 teaspoons of the peanut oil in same cleaned wok; add half of the
combined egg and water, swirl wok to make thin omelette. Cook, uncovered, until
egg is just set. Remove from wok; roll omelette, cut into thin strips. Heat 2 more
teaspoons of the peanut oil in wok; repeat process with remaining egg mixture.
5   Combine garlic, chillies, sugar, sauces and vinegar in small bowl; pour half of
the chilli mixture into small jug, reserve.
6   Combine pork in bowl with remaining half of the chilli mixture. Heat remaining
peanut oil in wok; stir-fry pork mixture about 5 minutes or until pork is cooked
through. Add prawns; stir-fry 1 minute. Add tofu; stir-fry, tossing gently to combine.
7   Remove wok from heat; add reserved chilli mixture and half of the onion, toss
to combine. Add vermicelli; toss gently to combine. Sprinkle with remaining
onion, omelette strips and coriander.

preparation time
35 minutes
(plus standing time)
cooking time
20 minutes
serves 4
per serving 20.7g total fat
(4.5g saturated fat); 1509kJ
(361 cal); 17.6g carbohydrate;
25.6g protein; 1.9g fibre

crab fried rice in omelette

¼ cup (60ml) peanut oil
4 green onions, chopped finely
2 fresh small red thai chillies,
  chopped finely
1 tablespoon red curry paste
  (page 174)
2 cups cooked jasmine rice

250g fresh crab meat
2 tablespoons lime juice
2 tablespoons fish sauce
8 eggs
2 tablespoons water
1 lime, cut into wedges

1 Heat 1 tablespoon of the oil in wok; stir-fry onion and chilli until onion softens. Add curry paste; stir-fry until mixture is fragrant.
2 Add rice; stir-fry until heated through. Remove from heat; place in large bowl. Add crab meat, juice and sauce; toss to combine.
3 Whisk eggs with the water in medium bowl. Heat about a quarter of the remaining oil in same cleaned wok; pour a quarter of the egg mixture into wok. Cook omelette, tilting pan, over low heat until egg is almost set. Spoon a quarter of the fried rice into centre of the omelette; using spatula, fold four sides of omelette over to enclose filling.
4 Press omelette firmly with spatula; turn carefully to brown other side. Remove omelette from wok; cover to keep warm. Repeat process with remaining oil, egg mixture and fried rice until you have four omelettes. Place omelettes on serving plate; serve with lime wedges.

preparation time
15 minutes
cooking time
25 minutes
serves 4
per serving 26.9g total fat
(6g saturated fat); 2930kJ
(701 cal); 83.7g carbohydrate;
29.4g protein; 1.9g fibre

chiang mai noodles

vegetable oil, for deep-frying
500g fresh egg noodles
1 large brown onion (200g),
    sliced thinly
2 green onions, sliced thinly
¼ cup loosely packed fresh
    coriander leaves
¼ cup (75g) red curry paste
    (page 174)
2 cloves garlic, crushed
¼ teaspoon ground turmeric

2 cups (500ml) water
400ml can coconut milk
500g chicken breast fillets,
    sliced thinly
¼ cup (60ml) fish sauce
1 tablespoon soy sauce
2 tablespoons grated palm sugar
2 teaspoons lime juice
2 tablespoons coarsely chopped
    fresh coriander
1 fresh long red thai chilli, sliced thinly

1 Heat oil in wok; deep-fry about 100g of the noodles, in batches, until crisp.
Drain on absorbent paper.
2 Using same heated oil, deep-fry brown onion, in batches, until browned lightly
and crisp. Drain on absorbent paper. Combine fried noodles, fried onion, green
onion and coriander leaves in small bowl. Discard oil from wok.
3 Place remaining noodles in large heatproof bowl, cover with boiling water;
use fork to separate noodles, drain.
4 Cook paste, garlic and turmeric in same cleaned wok, add the water and coconut
milk; bring to a boil, reduce heat, simmer, stirring, 2 minutes. Add chicken; cook,
stirring, about 5 minutes or until chicken is cooked through. Add sauces, sugar
and juice; cook, stirring, until sugar dissolves. Stir in chopped coriander.
5 Divide drained noodles among serving bowls. Spoon chicken curry mixture
into each bowl; top with fried noodle mixture, sprinkle with chilli slices.

Noodles were first introduced to Thailand by the Chinese,
who brought with them a number of types, including
vermicelli, rice and egg noodles. Also known as yellow
noodles, these are made from wheat flour and eggs,
sold fresh or dried, and range in size from fine strands
to pieces shoelace-thick. This noodle dish can be also
made vegetarian or with beef as well as chicken. Fresh
egg noodles can be purchased at any Asian grocer or
supermarket. They don't need to be cooked first, only
rinsed and soaked in hot water to remove any oil.

preparation time
20 minutes
cooking time
20 minutes
serves 4
per serving 34.7g total fat
(20.8g saturated fat); 3436kJ
(822 cal); 80.3g carbohydrate;
43.1g protein; 7.4g fibre

steamed jasmine rice

preparation time
1 minute
(plus standing time)
cooking time
12 minutes
serves 4
per serving 0.5g total fat
(0.1g saturated fat); 1480kJ
(354 cal); 79.1g carbohydrate;
6.6g protein; 0.9g fibre

2 cups (400g) jasmine rice

1 litre (4 cups) cold water

1 Combine rice and the water in large saucepan with a tight-fitting lid; bring
to a boil, stirring occasionally.
2 Reduce heat as low as possible; cook rice, covered tightly, about 12 minutes
or until all water is absorbed and rice is cooked as desired. Do not remove lid
or stir rice during cooking time. Remove from heat; stand, covered, 10 minutes
before serving.

black rice

preparation time
2 minutes
cooking time
20 minutes
serves 4
per serving 0.5g total fat
(0.1g saturated fat); 1480kJ
(354 cal); 79g carbohydrate;
6.6g protein; 0.8g fibre

2 cups (400g) black rice

1 Rinse rice in strainer under cold water until water runs clear.
2 Place rice in large saucepan of boiling water; boil, uncovered, stirring
occasionally, about 20 minutes or until rice is cooked as desired. Drain; stand,
covered, 10 minutes before serving.

glutinous rice

preparation time
10 minutes
(plus standing time)
cooking time
40 minutes
serves 4
per serving 0.5g total fat
(0.1g saturated fat); 1480kJ
(354 cal); 79.1g carbohydrate;
6.6g protein; 0.6g fibre

2 cups (400g) glutinous rice

1 Rinse rice in strainer under cold water until water runs clear. Soak rice in large
bowl of cold water overnight.
2 Drain rice. Line metal or bamboo steamer with muslin; place rice in steamer,
cover tightly. Place steamer over large saucepan of boiling water, taking care that
the bottom of the steamer does not touch the boiling water. Steam rice, tightly
covered, about 40 minutes or until cooked as desired. Do not remove lid or stir
rice during cooking time.

fried noodles with garlic pork

175g dried egg noodles
2 tablespoons peanut oil
2 cloves garlic, crushed
250g pork fillet, chopped finely
½ cup (70g) finely chopped peanuts
¼ cup (30g) dried shrimp
6 green onions, sliced thinly

2 tablespoons fish sauce
1 teaspoon grated palm sugar
1 fresh small red thai chilli,
  chopped finely
2 tablespoons lime juice
2 tablespoons finely chopped
  fresh coriander

preparation time
15 minutes
cooking time
15 minutes
serves 4
per serving 23.1g total fat
(4.7g saturated fat); 1885kJ
(451 cal); 34.6g carbohydrate;
24.5g protein; 3.4g fibre

1 Cook noodles in large saucepan of boiling water, uncovered, about 5 minutes
or until tender; drain well.
2 Heat oil in wok; stir-fry garlic and pork until pork is browned.
3 Add peanuts, shrimp, onion, sauce, sugar, chilli and juice; stir-fry 1 minute.
4 Stir in noodles and coriander, stir-fry until hot.

yellow coconut rice

1¾ cups (350g) long-grain white rice
1¼ cups (310ml) water
400ml can coconut cream
½ teaspoon salt

1 teaspoon white sugar
½ teaspoon ground turmeric
pinch saffron threads

preparation time
5 minutes
(plus standing time)
cooking time
15 minutes
serves 4
per serving 21.1g total fat
(18.2g saturated fat); 2186kJ
(523 cal); 73.9g carbohydrate;
7.7g protein; 2.4g fibre

1 Soak rice in large bowl of cold water 30 minutes. Pour rice into strainer; rinse
under cold water until water runs clear. Drain.
2 Place rice, the water, coconut cream, salt, sugar, turmeric and saffron in large
heavy-based saucepan; cover, bring to a boil, stirring occasionally. Reduce heat;
simmer, covered, without stirring, about 15 minutes or until rice is tender. Remove
from heat; stand, covered, 5 minutes.

คอน

SALADS

Assorted fresh vegetable leaves and herbs often accompany spicier Thai foods, but a salad itself is always one of the dishes served as part of a meal, to be eaten simultaneously with rice. Many salads have "yam" as part of their name, which loosely translates as "mix together different ingredients", the main one to be cooked and the others left crisp and fresh. Oil seldom appears in a dressing, which is to expressly combine the four tastes of Thai cooking: salty, hot, sweet and sour. Combinations of fish sauce, chilli, mint, thai basil and coriander are used to impart distinctive flavour to a salad.

char-grilled beef salad

¼ cup (60ml) fish sauce
¼ cup (60ml) lime juice
500g beef rump steak
3 lebanese cucumbers (390g),
  seeded, sliced thinly
4 fresh small red thai chillies,
  sliced thinly
4 green onions, sliced thinly
250g cherry tomatoes, halved

¼ cup firmly packed fresh
  vietnamese mint leaves
½ cup firmly packed fresh
  coriander leaves
½ cup firmly packed fresh
  thai basil leaves
1 tablespoon grated palm sugar
2 teaspoons soy sauce
1 clove garlic, crushed

1 Combine 2 tablespoons of the fish sauce and 1 tablespoon of the juice in medium bowl; add beef, toss to coat in marinade. Cover; refrigerate 3 hours or overnight.

2 Drain beef; discard marinade. Cook beef on heated oiled grill plate (or grill or barbecue) until cooked as desired. Cover beef; stand 5 minutes then slice beef thinly.

3 Meanwhile, combine cucumber, chilli, onion, tomato and herbs in large bowl.

4 Place sugar, soy sauce, garlic, remaining fish sauce and remaining juice in screw-top jar; shake well. Add beef and dressing to salad; toss gently to combine.

preparation time 25 minutes (plus refrigeration time)
cooking time 10 minutes
serves 4
per serving 8.7g total fat (3.8g saturated fat); 999kJ (239 cal); 7.9g carbohydrate; 30.7g protein; 2.9g fibre

calamari salad

1kg baby calamari
⅓ cup (80ml) water
1½ tablespoons fish sauce
2 tablespoons lime juice
1 fresh small red thai chilli,
    chopped finely
1 small white onion (80g), sliced thinly

10cm stick (20g) fresh lemon grass,
    chopped finely
1 tablespoon finely chopped
    fresh coriander
1 tablespoon finely chopped
    fresh mint
8 lettuce leaves

preparation time
50 minutes
cooking time
5 minutes
(plus cooling and
refrigeration time)
serves 4
per serving 1.5g total fat
(0.4g saturated fat); 439kJ
(105 cal); 2g carbohydrate;
19.7g protein; 1.9g fibre

1 Gently pull heads and entrails from calamari bodies; discard. Remove clear quills from inside bodies; discard. Remove side flaps and skin from calamari hoods; discard.

2 Cut hoods into 4cm squares, score inside surface of each square using a sharp knife.

3 Combine the water, sauce, juice and chilli in medium saucepan. Bring to a boil, add calamari; reduce heat, simmer, uncovered, about 2 minutes or until calamari is tender. Transfer mixture to bowl; cool.

4 Add onion, lemon grass, coriander and mint to bowl. Mix well; cover, refrigerate at least 1 hour. Serve salad on lettuce leaves.

cold prawn salad

200g bean thread noodles
1 clove garlic, crushed
2 tablespoons fish sauce
1 tablespoon lime juice
2 teaspoons peanut oil
¼ cup (35g) coarsely chopped
    roasted unsalted peanuts

2 green onions, sliced thinly
¼ cup coarsely chopped
    fresh coriander
2 fresh small red thai chillies,
    sliced thinly
1kg cooked large king prawns,
    peeled, deveined

preparation time
20 minutes
(plus standing time)
serves 4
per serving 7.2g total fat
(1.2g saturated fat); 1350kJ
(323 cal); 33.3g carbohydrate;
28.9g protein; 3.2g fibre

1 Place noodles in large heatproof bowl; cover with boiling water, stand until just tender, drain. Using kitchen scissors, cut noodles into random lengths.

2 Whisk garlic, sauce, juice and oil in large bowl.

3 Add noodles to bowl with nuts, onion, coriander, chilli and prawns; toss gently to combine.

crisp fish salad with chilli lime dressing

250g firm white fish fillets
vegetable oil, for deep-frying
1 medium red onion (170g),
 sliced thinly
6 green onions, sliced thinly
2 lebanese cucumbers (260g),
 seeded, sliced thinly
1 cup firmly packed thai mint leaves
1 cup firmly packed coriander leaves

2 tablespoons coarsely chopped
 roasted unsalted peanuts
2 teaspoons finely grated lime rind
chilli lime dressing
4 small green thai chillies, seeded,
 chopped finely
2 tablespoons fish sauce
⅓ cup (80ml) lime juice
1 tablespoon brown sugar

1   Preheat oven to moderate (180°C/160°C fan-forced).
2   Place ingredients for chilli lime dressing in screw-top jar; shake well.
3   Place fish on wire rack over oven tray; roast, uncovered, 20 minutes. When
cool enough to handle, cut fish into pieces, then blend or process, pulsing, until
mixture resembles coarse breadcrumbs.
4   Heat oil in wok; deep-fry fish, in batches, until browned lightly and crisp. Drain
on absorbent paper.
5   Combine onions, cucumber and herbs in large bowl; add chilli lime dressing,
toss to combine. Sprinkle salad with crisp fish, nuts and rind; serve immediately.

Thai mint (saranae), also known as marsh mint, is similar
to spearmint. Its somewhat thick round leaves are
usually used raw in salads or as a flavouring sprinkled
over soups. Available from Asian grocery stores.

preparation time
20 minutes
cooking time
30 minutes
serves 4
per serving 7.8g total fat
(1.3g saturated fat); 761kJ
(182 cal); 9.3g carbohydrate;
16.9g protein; 3.4g fibre

crab salad

500g fresh crab meat
250g chinese cabbage, chopped finely
1 lebanese cucumber (130g), seeded,
   chopped coarsely
1 medium red onion (170g), halved,
   sliced thinly
6 green onions, cut into 4cm lengths
1 cup loosely packed fresh thai
   mint leaves

dressing
2 cloves garlic, crushed
2 tablespoons lime juice
2 tablespoons fish sauce
1 tablespoon brown sugar
2 fresh small red thai chillies,
   chopped finely

preparation time
15 minutes
serves 4
per serving 1.1g total fat
(0.2g saturated fat); 560kJ
(134 cal); 10.3g carbohydrate;
18.9g protein; 3.4g fibre

1 Place ingredients for dressing in screw-top jar; shake well.
2 Drain crab in strainer; remove any shell; shred meat to desired texture.
3 Combine crab in large bowl with cabbage, cucumber, onions and mint; pour over dressing, toss to combine.

beef and mushroom salad

60g dried shiitake mushrooms
600g piece beef rump steak
2 tablespoons peanut oil
1 medium red capsicum (200g), sliced
½ cup (70g) roasted cashews
9 large spinach leaves, shredded

dressing
1 tablespoon sesame oil
2 tablespoons fish sauce
2 tablespoons sweet sherry
2 tablespoons oyster sauce

preparation time
25 minutes
(plus standing time)
cooking time
10 minutes
(plus cooling time)
serves 4
per serving 32.7g total fat
(8.3g saturated fat); 2094kJ
(501 cal); 9g carbohydrate;
39.5g protein; 2.6g fibre

1 Place mushrooms in medium heatproof bowl; cover with warm water, stand 20 minutes. Drain mushrooms, discard stems; cut caps into thin slices.
2 Combine ingredients for dressing in small bowl; mix well.
3 Trim excess fat from beef. Heat oil in large frying pan; cook beef until browned both sides and cooked as desired. Cover beef; stand 10 minutes, slice beef thinly.
4 Combine beef, mushrooms, capsicum, nuts and spinach in large bowl. Pour over dressing; toss to combine.

minced pork salad with ginger and mint larb

500g pork fillet, chopped
1 tablespoon peanut oil
1 tablespoon water
¼ cup (60ml) lime juice
2 tablespoons fish sauce
2 fresh small red thai chillies,
   chopped finely
1 small brown onion (80g), sliced thinly
4 green onions, chopped finely
¼ cup (35g) peanuts
4cm piece fresh ginger (20g),
   grated finely

2 tablespoons finely chopped
   fresh mint
2 tablespoons fresh coriander leaves
8 cos lettuce leaves
1 tablespoon coarsely chopped
   peanuts, extra
4cm piece fresh ginger (20g), cut
   into thin strips
2 tablespoons fresh coriander
   leaves, extra

1 Process pork until finely minced. Heat oil in large frying pan; cook pork and water, stirring, until pork is tender.

2 Remove pork from heat, stir in juice, sauce and chilli; cool.

3 Combine pork mixture with onions, nuts, grated ginger, mint and coriander in large bowl.

4 Serve pork salad over lettuce; sprinkle with extra chopped nuts, ginger strips and extra coriander.

Also known as romaine, cos is the traditional Caesar salad lettuce, but its pale green, long tapering leaves make it a perfect vehicle to use as an edible salad plate for this savoury pork mixture (called "larb muu" in Thai). Baby cos lettuce leaves are fabulous used as the base for many different finger foods: they not only hold each canapé but they can be consumed as well.

preparation time
20 minutes
cooking time
10 minutes
(plus cooling time)
serves 4
per serving 20.3g total fat
(5g saturated fat); 1396kJ
(334 cal); 4.8g carbohydrate;
31.7g protein; 3.1g fibre

pork and lychee salad

1 tablespoon peanut oil
300g pork fillet
565g can lychees, rinsed,
    drained, halved
1 medium red capsicum (200g),
    sliced thinly
10cm stick (20g) fresh lemon grass,
    chopped finely
2 fresh kaffir lime leaves,
    shredded finely
100g watercress
2 tablespoons coarsely chopped
    fresh vietnamese mint
2 tablespoons drained thinly sliced
    pickled ginger
2 tablespoons fried shallot

pickled garlic dressing
1 tablespoon drained finely
    chopped pickled garlic
2 fresh small red thai chillies,
    sliced thinly
1 tablespoon rice vinegar
1 tablespoon lime juice
1 tablespoon fish sauce
1 tablespoon grated palm sugar

1 Place ingredients for picked garlic dressing in screw-top jar; shake well.
2 Heat oil in wok; cook pork until browned all over and cooked through. Cover pork; stand 10 minutes then slice pork thinly. Place pork in medium bowl with pickled garlic dressing; toss to coat pork all over. Stand 10 minutes.
3 Meanwhile, combine lychees, capsicum, lemon grass, lime leaves, watercress and mint in large bowl.
4 Add pork mixture to lychee mixture; toss gently to combine. Serve sprinkled with pickled ginger and fried shallot.

If fresh lychees are available when you're making this salad, substitute about 300g of these for the canned variety: just peel and halve them. You can also replace the lychees with rambutans or longans in this salad for Thai authenticity. Fruit is used in many savoury dishes in Thailand, far more than in the West, and the exotic flavours of tropical fruits are one of the identifiable signs of a fresh Thai salad or even stir-fry.

preparation time
20 minutes
(plus standing time)
cooking time
10 minutes
serves 4
per serving 11.2g total fat
(2.9g saturated fat); 1179kJ
(282 cal); 24.4g carbohydrate;
18.8g protein; 3.8g fibre

spicy chicken salad *larb gai*

2 tablespoons long-grain white rice
1 tablespoon peanut oil
10cm stick (20g) fresh lemon grass,
    chopped finely
2 fresh small red thai chillies,
    chopped finely
2 cloves garlic, crushed
1 tablespoon finely chopped
    fresh galangal
750g chicken mince
1 lebanese cucumber (130g),
    seeded, sliced thinly
1 small red onion (100g), sliced thinly

100g bean sprouts
½ cup loosely packed fresh
    thai basil leaves
1 cup loosely packed fresh
    coriander leaves
4 large iceberg lettuce leaves
dressing
⅓ cup (80ml) lime juice
2 tablespoons fish sauce
2 tablespoons kecap manis
2 tablespoons peanut oil
2 teaspoons grated palm sugar
½ teaspoon sambal oelek

1 Heat dry wok; stir-fry rice until browned lightly. Blend or process (or crush using mortar and pestle) rice until it resembles fine breadcrumbs.
2 Place ingredients for dressing in screw-top jar; shake well.
3 Heat oil in wok; stir-fry lemon grass, chilli, garlic and galangal until fragrant. Remove from wok. Stir-fry chicken, in batches, until changed in colour and cooked through.
4 Return chicken and lemon grass mixture to wok with about one-third of the dressing; stir-fry about 5 minutes or until mixture thickens slightly.
5 Place remaining dressing in large bowl with chicken, cucumber, onion, sprouts and herbs; toss gently to combine. Place lettuce leaves on serving plates; divide larb among leaves, sprinkle with ground rice.

Bean sprouts, also known as bean shoots, are the tender new growths of assorted beans and seeds germinated for consumption as sprouts. The most readily available are mung beans, soy beans, alfalfa and snow pea sprouts. In Thailand, the tiny root hanging off the end of every sprout is picked off, but this tedious job is certainly unnecessary for the taste of this delicious warm chicken salad.

preparation time
25 minutes
cooking time
20 minutes
serves 4
per serving 21.8g total fat
(4.7g saturated fat); 1772kJ
(424 cal); 12.3g carbohydrate;
43g protein; 3.1g fibre

One of the many interesting things about Thai cooking is the use of tropical or unusual fruits in its main courses, salads or side dishes. Banana, mango, pawpaw and pomelo are just a few of the fruits that find their way out of the dessert fruit platter. Here, where pomelo is married with peanuts and splashed with a tart, garlicky dressing, you'll experience a wonderful taste sensation outside the realm of western familiarity, but one which is delightfully more-ish.

cabbage salad with lime juice dressing

3 fresh large red chillies
2 tablespoons peanut oil
6 cloves garlic, sliced thinly
6 green onions, sliced thinly
½ medium cabbage (750g), shredded
1 tablespoon crushed peanuts

dressing
2 tablespoons fish sauce
2 tablespoons lime juice
½ cup (125ml) coconut milk

preparation time
10 minutes
cooking time
10 minutes
serves 6
per serving 10.7g total fat
(4.9g saturated fat); 585kJ
(140 cal); 5.3g carbohydrate;
3.3g protein; 5.7g fibre

1 Combine dressing ingredients in small bowl; mix well.
2 Cut chillies into thin strips lengthways. Heat oil in medium frying pan; cook chilli, garlic and onion, separately, until browned lightly and crisp; drain on absorbent paper.
3 Add cabbage to large saucepan of boiling water; drain immediately.
4 Combine cabbage and dressing in large bowl; mix well. Serve salad topped with stir-fried chilli mixture and peanuts.

pomelo salad

1 small red onion (100g)
4 large pomelos (4kg)
2 green onions, sliced thinly
2 fresh small red thai chillies, sliced thinly
¼ cup coarsely chopped fresh coriander

½ cup (70g) coarsely chopped roasted unsalted peanuts
2 cloves garlic, crushed
1 tablespoon grated palm sugar
¼ cup (60ml) lime juice
1 tablespoon soy sauce

preparation time
20 minutes
cooking time
15 minutes
serves 4
per serving 9.7g total fat
(1.2g saturated fat); 1241kJ
(297 cal); 38.1g carbohydrate;
11.2g protein; 6.2g fibre

1 Halve red onion; cut each half into paper-thin wedges.
2 Peel and carefully segment pomelos; discard membranes. Combine segments in large bowl with onions, chilli, coriander and nuts.
3 Combine remaining ingredients in small jug; stir until sugar dissolves. Pour dressing over pomelo mixture; toss gently to combine.

green papaya salad

100g snake beans
850g green papaya
250g cherry tomatoes, quartered
3 small green thai chillies,
    chopped finely
2 tablespoons finely chopped
    dried shrimp
¼ cup (60ml) lime juice
1 tablespoon fish sauce

1 tablespoon grated palm sugar
2 cloves garlic, crushed
¼ cup coarsely chopped
    fresh coriander
2 cups (120g) finely shredded
    iceberg lettuce
⅓ cup (45g) coarsely chopped
    roasted unsalted peanuts

1 Cut beans in 5cm pieces; cut pieces in half lengthways. Boil, steam or microwave beans until just tender. Drain, rinse under cold water; drain.
2 Meanwhile, peel papaya. Quarter lengthways, remove seeds; grate papaya coarsely.
3 Place papaya and beans in large bowl with tomato, chilli and shrimp. Add combined juice, sauce, sugar, garlic and half of the coriander; toss gently to combine.
4 Place lettuce on serving plates; spoon papaya salad over lettuce, sprinkle with nuts and remaining coriander.

Green (unripe) papayas are readily available in various sizes at many Asian shops and markets. Select one that is very hard and slightly shiny, which indicates that it is freshly picked. It's imperative that it be totally unripe – the flesh so light green it is almost white. A firm papaya will soften rapidly if you don't use it within one or two days. Green papaya has very little taste, but acts as a sponge to absorb the combined thai flavours (hot, sour, sweet and salty) of the other ingredients. Assemble the salad just before you want to serve it.

preparation time
15 minutes
cooking time
15 minutes
serves 4
per serving 5.7g total fat (0.8g saturated fat); 648kJ (155 cal); 16.9g carbohydrate; 5.5g protein; 7g fibre

tofu and egg salad

2 teaspoons chopped fresh
  coriander root
1 clove garlic, crushed
4cm piece fresh ginger (20g),
  grated finely
2 tablespoons brown sugar
2 tablespoons dark soy sauce
1 teaspoon five-spice powder
2 teaspoons peanut oil

¼ cup (60ml) water
6 radishes (200g)
375g fresh firm silken tofu,
  drained, cubed
1 tablespoon chopped fresh
  coriander leaves
1 fresh small red thai chilli,
  chopped finely
1 hard-boiled egg, chopped

preparation time
25 minutes
(plus standing time)
cooking time
15 minutes
(plus cooling time)
serves 4
per serving 10.1g total fat
(1.8g saturated fat); 777kJ
(186 cal); 9g carbohydrate;
13.8g protein; 2.5g fibre

1   Blend or process coriander root, garlic, ginger, sugar, sauce and five-spice powder until well combined.
2   Heat oil in small saucepan, add coriander mixture; cook, stirring, about 2 minutes or until fragrant. Stir in water; cool to room temperature.
3   Cut radishes into thin strips. Combine tofu and radish in bowl, pour over coriander mixture; cover, stand 2 hours, stirring occasionally.
4   Drain tofu mixture, combine with coriander leaves, chilli and egg.

spicy tofu salad

750g fresh firm silken tofu
1 small red onion (100g), halved
1 medium carrot (120g)
1 medium green capsicum (200g)
2 tablespoons peanuts,
  chopped coarsely

dressing
2 fresh small red thai chillies,
  chopped finely
¼ cup (60ml) lime juice
2 tablespoons brown sugar
1 tablespoon fish sauce
10cm stick (20g) fresh lemon grass,
  chopped finely

preparation time
20 minutes
(plus standing and
refrigeration time)
serves 6
per serving 10.3g total fat
(1.5g saturated fat); 849kJ
(203 cal); 8.9g carbohydrate;
16.9g protein; 3.6g fibre

1   Place dressing ingredients in screw-top jar; shake well.
2   Pat tofu with absorbent paper; cut into 1cm pieces. Spread tofu, in single layer, on absorbent-paper-lined tray; cover tofu with more absorbent paper, stand at least 20 minutes.
3   Slice onion thinly. Cut carrot and capsicum into thin strips.
4   Combine tofu, onion, carrot, capsicum and dressing in medium bowl; mix well. Cover, refrigerate 3 hours. Serve salad sprinkled with peanuts.

CURRY PASTES

red curry

20 dried long red chillies
1 teaspoon ground coriander
2 teaspoons ground cumin
1 teaspoon hot paprika
2cm piece fresh ginger (10g),
   chopped finely
3 large cloves garlic, quartered
1 medium red onion (170g),
   chopped coarsely

2 x 10cm sticks (40g) fresh
   lemon grass, chopped finely
1 fresh kaffir lime leaf, sliced thinly
2 tablespoons coarsely chopped fresh
   coriander root and stem mixture
2 teaspoons shrimp paste
1 tablespoon peanut oil

preparation time
20 minutes
(plus standing time)
cooking time
3 minutes
makes 1 cup (300g)
per tablespoon
1.6g total fat
(0.3g saturated fat); 92kJ
(22 cal); 1.2g carbohydrate;
0.4g protein; 0.5g fibre

1 Place whole chillies in small heatproof jug, cover with boiling water; stand 15 minutes, drain.

2 Meanwhile, dry-fry ground coriander, cumin and paprika over medium heat in small frying pan, stirring until fragrant.

3 Blend or process chillies and roasted spices with remaining ingredients, except for the oil, until mixture forms a paste, pausing to scrape down sides of machine occasionally during blending.

4 Add oil to paste mixture; continue to blend until smooth.

green curry

2 teaspoons ground coriander
2 teaspoons ground cumin
10 long green chillies,
   chopped coarsely
10 small green chillies,
   chopped coarsely
1 large clove garlic, quartered
4 green onions, chopped coarsely
10cm stick (20g) fresh lemon grass,
   chopped finely

2 fresh kaffir lime leaves, sliced thinly
1 teaspoon finely chopped
   fresh galangal
¼ cup coarsely chopped fresh
   coriander root and stem mixture
1 teaspoon shrimp paste
1 tablespoon peanut oil

preparation time
20 minutes
cooking time
3 minutes
makes 1½ cups (450g)
per tablespoon
1g total fat
(0.2g saturated fat); 46kJ
(11 cal); 0.2g carbohydrate;
0.2g protein; 0.2g fibre

1 Dry-fry ground coriander and cumin in small frying pan over medium heat, stirring until fragrant.

2 Blend or process roasted spices with remaining ingredients, except for the oil, until mixture forms a paste.

3 Add oil to paste mixture; continue to blend until smooth.

yellow curry

1 teaspoon ground coriander
1 teaspoon ground cumin
½ teaspoon ground cinnamon
1 teaspoon finely chopped
   fresh turmeric
5 fresh long yellow chillies,
   chopped coarsely
2 large cloves garlic, quartered
1 medium brown onion (150g),
   chopped coarsely

10cm stick (20g) fresh lemon grass,
   chopped finely
2 teaspoons finely chopped
   fresh galangal
1 tablespoon coarsely chopped fresh
   coriander root and stem mixture
1 teaspoon shrimp paste
1 tablespoon peanut oil

preparation time
20 minutes
cooking time
3 minutes
makes 1 cup (300g)
per tablespoon
1.6g total fat
(0.3g saturated fat); 79kJ
(19 cal); 0.8g carbohydrate;
0.3g protein; 0.3g fibre

1 Dry-fry ground coriander, cumin and cinnamon in small frying pan over medium heat, stirring until fragrant.
2 Blend or process roasted spices with remaining ingredients, except for the oil, until mixture forms a paste.
3 Add oil to paste mixture; continue to blend until smooth.

panang curry

25 dried long red chillies
1 teaspoon ground coriander
2 teaspoons ground cumin
2 large cloves garlic, quartered
8 green onions, chopped coarsely
2 x 10cm sticks (40g) fresh
   lemon grass, chopped finely

2 teaspoons finely chopped
   fresh galangal
2 teaspoons shrimp paste
½ cup (70g) roasted unsalted peanuts
2 tablespoons peanut oil

preparation time
20 minutes
(plus standing time)
cooking time
3 minutes
makes 1 cup (300g)
per tablespoon
5.9g total fat
(1g saturated fat); 276kJ
(66 cal); 1.2g carbohydrate;
1.8g protein; 0.9g fibre

1 Place whole chillies in small heatproof jug, cover with boiling water; stand 15 minutes, drain.
2 Meanwhile, dry-fry ground coriander and cumin in small frying pan over medium heat, stirring until fragrant.
3 Blend or process chillies and roasted spices with remaining ingredients, except for the oil, until mixture forms a paste.
4 Add oil to paste mixture; continue to blend until smooth.

note Keep curry paste, covered tightly, in the refrigerator for up to a week.
You could also use a mortar and pestle to combine the ingredients for the paste.
Freeze any leftover paste for up to three months. Place tablespoons of curry paste
in an ice-cube tray, wrap the tray tightly in plactic wrap and freeze the paste. Once
frozen, remove the blocks of curry paste, then re-wrap them individually and return
to the freezer until required.

GLOSSARY

chinese cabbage

opal basil

thai basil

bok choy

dried chilli flakes

coriander

arrowroot a starch used mostly for thickening. Cornflour can be substituted, for arrowroot, but it will not give as clear a glaze.

bamboo shoots tender shoots of bamboo plants, available in cans; drain and rinse before use.

BASIL

opal: has large purple leaves and a sweet, almost gingery flavour; has better keeping properties than most basils. It can be used instead of thai basil, but not holy basil, in recipes.

holy: also known as kra pao or hot basil, has a hot, spicy flavour similar to clove.

thai: also known as horapa, is different from holy basil and sweet basil in both look and taste, having smaller leaves and purplish stems. It has a slight licorice or aniseed taste.

bean sprouts also known as bean shoots; tender new growths of assorted beans and seeds germinated for consumption. They include mung beans, soy beans, snow pea sprouts and alfalfa.

bok choy also known as bak choy, pak choi, chinese white cabbage or chinese chard, has a fresh, mild mustard taste; use stems and leaves. *Baby bok choy,* also known as shanghai bok choy, chinese chard, white cabbage or pak kat farang, is small and more tender than bok choy.

BREADCRUMBS

packaged: fine-textured, crunchy, purchased white breadcrumbs.

stale: one- or two-day-old bread made into crumbs by blending or processing.

butter use unsalted (sweet) or salted; 125g is equal to 1 stick butter.

capsicum also known as bell pepper or, simply, pepper.

cardamom purchase in pod, seed or ground form. Has a distinctive aromatic, sweetly rich flavour.

CHILLI available in many types and sizes. Use rubber gloves when seeding and chopping fresh chillies as they can burn your skin. To lessen the heat level, remove the seeds and membranes.

dried flakes: deep-red, dehydrated, extremely fine slices and whole seeds. Use in cooking, or sprinkle over food in the same way as salt and pepper.

powder: the Asian variety is the hottest, made from dried ground thai chillies; can be used as a substitute for fresh chillies in the proportion of ½ teaspoon ground chilli powder to 1 medium chopped fresh chilli.

sweet chilli sauce: the comparatively mild thai sauce made from red chillies, sugar, garlic and vinegar; used more as a condiment than in cooking.

thai: small, medium hot, and bright red in colour.

chinese broccoli also known as gai larn, kanah, chinese kale and gai lum; appreciated more for its stems than its coarse leaves.

chinese cabbage this is the most common cabbage in South-East Asia; also known as peking or napa cabbage, wong bok or petsai. It is elongated in shape with pale green, crinkly leaves.

COCONUT

cream: made commercially from the first pressing of the coconut flesh alone, without the addition of water; the second pressing (less rich) is sold as the milk. Available at supermarkets in cans and cartons.

desiccated: unsweetened, concentrated, dried, finely shredded coconut.

milk: not the juice found inside the fruit, which is known as coconut water, but the diluted liquid from the second pressing from the white meat of a mature coconut (the first pressing produces coconut cream). Available in cartons and cans at supermarkets.

shredded: thin strips of dried coconut.

coriander also known as cilantro, chinese parsley or pak chee; bright green-leafed herb with a pungent flavour. Often stirred into or sprinkled over a dish just before serving. Both the stems and roots are also used in Thai cooking; wash well before chopping.

thai eggplant

dried shrimp

pea eggplant

fish sauce

five spice

fried garlic

galangal

cornflour a thickening agent used in cooking, also known as cornstarch; used similarly to arrowroot.

cumin also known as zeera.

curry powder a blend of ground spices used for convenience when making Indian food. May consist of some of the following spices in varying proportions: dried chilli, cinnamon, coriander, cumin, fennel, fenugreek, cardamom, turmeric and mace. Available in mild or hot varieties.

dried shrimp (goong hang) salted sun-dried prawns that range in size from not much larger than a rice seed to about 1cm in length. They are sold, shelled as a rule, in packages in all Asian grocery stores.

EGGPLANT a purple-skinned vegetable also known as aubergine.

eggplant, pea: also known as makeua puong; are sold fresh, in bunches like grapes, or pickled in jars. Are more bitter than the slightly larger thai eggplants. Found in Asian grocery stores.

eggplant, thai: also known as makeua prao; golf-ball sized eggplants available in different colours, but most commonly green traced in off-white. They have bitter seeds that must be removed before using. Found in Asian grocery stores.

eggs some recipes call for raw or barely cooked eggs; exercise caution if there is a salmonella problem in your area.

fish fillets any boneless firm white fish fillet can be used; blue eye, bream, swordfish, whiting, ling or sea perch are all good choices. Check for any small pieces of bone in the fillets and use tweezers to remove them.

fish sauce labelled naam pla if it is Thai made; the Vietnamese version, nuoc naam, is almost identical. Made from pulverised salted fermented fish (most often anchovies), and has a pungent smell and strong taste. There are many types of fish sauce of varying intensity on the market, so use according to your taste.

five-spice powder a fragrant mixture of cloves, ground cinnamon, star anise, sichuan pepper and fennel seeds. Also known as chinese five-spice.

FLOUR
plain: an all-purpose flour, made from wheat.

self-raising: plain flour sifted with baking powder in the proportion of 1 cup flour to 2 teaspoons baking powder.

fried garlic (kratiem jiew) is used as a condiment on the table or sprinkled over cooked dishes. Can be purchased canned or in cellophane bags at Asian grocery stores. Once opened, leftovers will keep for months if tightly sealed. Make your own by slicing garlic thinly and shallow-frying in vegetable oil until golden-brown and crisp.

fried onion sold in Asian grocery stores packed in jars or in cellophane bags; is used as a topping for various thai rice and noodle dishes, and also served as a condiment as part of a Thai meal.

fried shallot (homm jiew) is used as a condiment on the table or sprinkled over cooked dishes. Can be purchased canned or in cellophane bags at Asian grocery stores; once opened, leftovers will keep for months if tightly sealed.

galangal also known as ka, a rhizome with a hot ginger-citrusy flavour; used similarly to ginger and garlic as a seasoning and ingredient. Sometimes known as thai, siamese or laos ginger. It also comes in a dried powdered form called laos. Fresh ginger can be substituted for fresh galangal, but the flavour of the dish will not be the same.

gelatine we used powdered gelatine; it is also available in sheet form known as leaf gelatine.

GINGER also known as green or root ginger; the thick gnarled root of a tropical plant. Can be kept, peeled, covered with dry sherry, in a jar and refrigerated, or frozen in an airtight container.

pickled pink: available, packaged, from Asian grocery stores; pickled, paper-thin shavings of ginger in a mixture of vinegar, sugar and natural colouring.

gow-gee wrappers also known as gow-gee pastry. Egg pastry sheets or spring roll or wonton wrappers can be substituted.

hoisin sauce a thick, sweet and spicy chinese sauce made from salted fermented soy beans, garlic, and onions. Used as a baste, marinade or in stir-fries.

ka chai (can be spelled krachai or kah chi) is also known as lesser galangal, chinese ginger or finger-root. Similar to ginger in flavour with a slight hint of camphor; it is available from Asian grocery stores.

kaffir lime also known as magrood, leech lime or jeruk purut. Bumpy-skinned, wrinkled green fruit of a small citrus tree originally grown in South Africa and South-East Asia; usually only the zest is used.

kaffir lime leaves also known as bai magrood; look like two glossy dark green leaves joined end to end, forming a rounded hourglass shape. Used fresh or dried in many Asian dishes, and used like bay leaves or curry leaves, especially in Thai cooking. Sold fresh, dried or frozen, the dried leaves are less potent so double the number called for in a recipe if you substitute them for fresh leaves. A strip of fresh lime peel can be substituted for each kaffir lime leaf.

kecap manis also known as ketjap manis or sieu wan; a dark, thick, sweet soy sauce used in most South-East Asian cooking. There is no real substitute, but dissolving some brown sugar in soy sauce will suffice.

kumara Polynesian name of orange-fleshed sweet potato often confused with yam.

lebanese cucumber short, slender and thin-skinned; this variety is also known as the european cucumber or the burpless cucumber.

lemon grass a clumping, tall, lemon-smelling and tasting, sharp-edged grass; the white lower part of the stem is used, finely chopped, in cooking.

manjo mirin a seasoned, sweet Japanese cooking wine; made of water, rice, corn syrup and alcohol.

mince also known as ground meat; can be beef, pork, lamb or poultry.

mint, vietnamese also known as rau ram, cambodian mint, pak pai, laksa leaf and daun kesom. Not a mint at all, but a pungent and peppery narrow-leafed member of the buckwheat family.

MUSHROOMS

button: small, cultivated white mushrooms with a mild flavour.

shiitake: when fresh are also known as golden oak, forest or chinese black mushrooms; although cultivated, have the earthiness and taste of wild mushrooms. When dried, are known as donko or dried chinese mushrooms; rehydrate before use.

straw: also known as paddy straw or grass mushrooms; seldom available fresh, but easily found canned or dried in Asian grocery stores. Straw mushrooms have an intense earthy flavour.

NOODLES

bean thread: also known as wun sen or cellophane or glass noodles because they're transparent when they're cooked; made from extruded mung bean paste. White in colour (not off-white like rice vermicelli), very delicate and fine; available dried in various size bundles. Must be soaked to soften before use; using them deep-fried requires no pre-soaking.

egg: also known as ba mee or yellow noodles; made from wheat flour and eggs. Sold fresh or dried; range in size from very fine strands to wide, spaghetti-like pieces as thick as a shoelace.

fried: crispy wheat noodles packaged (most commonly in a 100g packet) already deep-fried and sometimes labelled "crunchy noodles".

kaffir lime

ka chai

kaffir lime leaves

kumara

vietnamese mint

shiitake

fresh rice: can be found under various names – ho fun, sen yau, pho or kway tiau – depending on the manufacturer. They can be purchased in various widths or, more commonly, in tea-towel-size sheets weighing about 500g each, which you cut into the noodle width you prefer. These noodles do not need pre-cooking, but do require a hot-water "bath" in order to separate them into individual strands before draining and frying.

rice stick: also known as sen lek, ho fun or kway teow. Very popular South-East Asian dried rice noodles; come in different widths and should be soaked in hot water until soft.

OIL

peanut: made from ground peanuts; most commonly used oil in Asian cooking because of its high smoke point (capacity to handle high heat without burning).

sesame: made from roasted, crushed white sesame seeds; a flavouring rather than a cooking medium.

vegetable: any of a number of oils sourced from plants rather than animal fats.

ONION

brown and white: are interchangeable. Their pungent flesh adds flavour to a vast range of dishes.

green: also known as scallion or, incorrectly, shallot; an immature onion picked before the bulb has formed, having a long, bright-green edible stalk.

red: also known as spanish, red spanish or bermuda onion; a sweet-flavoured, large, purple-red onion.

shallot: also called french shallots, golden shallots or eschalots; small, elongated, brown-skinned members of the onion family. Grows in clusters similar to garlic.

oyster sauce Asian in origin, this rich, brown sauce is made from oysters and their brine, cooked with salt and soy sauce, and thickened with starches.

paprika ground dried red capsicum (bell pepper); available smoked, sweet or hot.

patty-pan squash also known as crookneck or custard marrow pumpkins; a round, slightly flat summer squash being yellow to pale green in colour and having a scalloped edge. Harvested young, it has a firm white flesh and a distinct flavour.

peanut butter peanuts that have been ground into a paste; available in crunchy and smooth varieties.

pickled galangal (ka dong) is used both in cooking and as a condiment to be served with various dishes. It is sold in jars or in cryovac packs from Asian grocery stores. You can substitute pickled ginger, but the taste will differ.

pickled garlic sweet and subtle pickled garlic, or kratiem dong, is the young green bulb packed whole and unpeeled in brine. Use in cooking, or sprinkled over noodle or rice dishes.

pickled ginger can be used both in cooking and as a condiment. Available in jars or cryovac packs from Asian grocery stores.

pickled green peppercorns we used pickled thai green peppercorns, which are canned, still strung in clusters, but you can use an equivalent weight from a bottle of green peppercorns in brine. Without separating them from their strings, rinse and dry before using.

pickled ka chai (can be spelled krachai or kah chi) is also known as lesser galangal. Similar to ginger in flavour with a slight hint of camphor, it is available from Asian supermarkets and greengrocers.

pomelo similar to grapefruit in many ways, a pomelo is sweeter, somewhat more conical in shape and slightly larger, about the size of a small coconut.

prawns also known as shrimp.

preserved turnip (hua chai po or cu cai muoi on the label) is also called dried radish because it is very similar to dried daikon. It is very salty, and should be rinsed and dried well before being used in cooking.

lemon grass

rice stick noodles

pickled galangal

patty pan squash

pomelo

preserved turnip

prawn

star anise

seafood sticks

saffron

spring roll wrappers

sambal oelek

palm sugar

puff pastry, ready-rolled packaged sheets of frozen puff pastry, available from supermarkets.

RICE

black: also known as purple rice because, although a deep charcoal when raw, after cooking it turns a purplish-black colour. A medium-grain unmilled rice, with a white kernel under the black bran, it has a nutty, whole-grain flavour and is crunchy to the bite, similar to wild rice.

glutinous: a thai glutinous rice that is also known as "sweet" or "sticky" rice. It is a uniquely flavoured rice that is eaten, formed into small balls, with the fingers and dipped into savoury dishes to soak up their sauces. The grains are short, fat and chalky white in the centre; when cooked they become soft and sticky. Glutinous rice is a particular variety of rice that requires long soaking and steaming; other varieties of rice cannot be cooked by this method successfully.

jasmine: thai jasmine rice is recognised around the world as having a particular aromatic quality that can almost be described as perfumed or floral. A long-grained white rice, it is sometimes used in place of the more-expensive basmati rice in South-East Asia. Jasmine rice is rather moist in texture and clings together after cooking; adding salt during cooking is not recommended because it destroys the delicate flavour of the rice. No Thai meal is complete without a large bowl of hot jasmine rice on the table.

long-grain: elongated grain, remains separate when cooked; most popular steaming rice in Asia.

short-grain: a fat, almost round grain with a high starch content; grains clump together when cooked.

rose water extract (called gulab in India) made from crushed rose petals; used for its aromatic quality in many sweetmeats (any type of sweet food made of sugar) and desserts.

saffron stigma of a member of the crocus family, it is available in strands or ground form. Once infused, it imparts a yellow-orange colour to food. Quality varies greatly; the best is the most expensive spice in the world. Should be stored in the freezer.

sambal oelek also ulek or olek; Indonesian in origin; a salty paste made from ground chillies and vinegar.

seafood sticks also known as crab sticks. Made from processed Alaskan pollack flavoured with crab.

shrimp paste also known as belacan. Dried shrimp paste is sold in slabs or flat cakes.

soy sauce also known as sieu; is made from fermented soy beans. Several types are available in most supermarkets and Asian food stores.

spinach known as english spinach and, incorrectly, silver beet. Tender green leaves are good uncooked in salads or added to soups, stir-fries and stews just before serving.

spring roll wrappers also called egg roll wrappers; they come in various sizes and can be purchased fresh or frozen from Asian grocery stores. Made from a delicate wheat-based pastry, they also can be used for making samosas and gow gees.

star anise a dried star-shaped pod whose seeds have an astringent aniseed flavour; used to favour stocks and marinades.

SUGAR

brown: an extremely soft, fine granulated sugar retaining molasses for its colour and flavour.

caster: also known as superfine or finely granulated table sugar.

palm: also known as nam tan pip, jaggery, jawa or gula melaka; made from the sap of the sugar palm tree. Light brown to black in colour and usually sold in rock-hard cakes; substitute palm sugar with brown sugar, if unavailable.

raw: natural brown granulated sugar.

sugar snap peas

tamarind

tofu

tamarind concentrate

wonton wrappers

water chestnuts (fresh)

white: we used coarse, granulated table sugar, also known as crystal sugar.

sweetened condensed milk from which 60% of the water has been removed; the remaining milk is then sweetened with sugar.

sugar snap peas also known as honey snap peas; fresh small pea that can be eaten whole, pod and all, similarly to snow peas.

tamarind from the same family as various beans, the tamarind tree is native to tropical Africa and, more recently, South-East Asia. The tree can grow as high as 25 metres, and produces clusters of brown "hairy" pods, each of which is filled with seeds and a viscous pulp that are dried and pressed into the blocks of tamarind found in Asian grocery stores. Tamarind gives a sweet-sour, slightly astringent taste to food. An important ingredient in Thai, Indian and other Asian cuisines, tamarind is used mainly as a souring agent in marinades, pastes, sauces and dressings.

tamarind concentrate (or paste) is the commercial result of the distillation of tamarind juice into a condensed, compacted paste. Thick and purplish-black, it is ready to use, with no soaking or straining required; dilute with water according to taste. Add to to marinades and chutneys.

thai shallots, purple (homm) are also called asian or pink shallots; used throughout South-East Asia, they are a member of the onion family, but resemble garlic in that they grow in multiple-clove bulbs. They are intensely flavoured, and are eaten fresh or deep-fried as a condiment as well as used pounded in curry pastes or tossed through stir-fries.

tofu (tao hu) also known as bean curd, an off-white, custard-like product made from the "milk" of crushed soy beans; comes fresh as soft or firm, and processed as fried or pressed dried sheets. Leftover fresh tofu can be refrigerated in water (which is changed daily) for up to four days.

tofu, silken refers to the manufacturing method of straining the soy bean liquid through silk.

TOMATO
paste: triple-concentrated tomato puree used to flavour soups, stews, sauces and casseroles.

sauce: also known as catsup or ketchup; a flavoured condiment made from pureed tomatoes, vinegar and spices.

cherry: also known as tiny tim or tom thumb tomatoes; small and round.

turmeric also known as kamin, is a rhizome related to galangal and ginger. It must be grated or pounded to release its somewhat acrid aroma and pungent flavour. Known for the golden colour it imparts to the dishes of which it's a part, fresh turmeric can be substituted with the more common dried powder (use 2 teaspoons of ground turmeric plus a teaspoon of sugar for every 20g of fresh turmeric called for in a recipe).

VINEGAR
rice: a colourless vinegar made from fermented rice and flavoured with sugar and salt. Also known as seasoned rice vinegar. Sherry can be substituted.
rice wine: made from fermented rice.
white: made from spirit of cane sugar.

water chestnuts resemble the chestnut in appearance, hence the English name. Small brown tubers with a crisp, white, nutty-tasting flesh. They are best eaten fresh, however, canned water chestnuts are more easily obtained and can be kept about a month, under refrigeration, once opened.

wonton wrappers also known as wonton skins. Sold packaged in large amounts and found in the refrigerated section of Asian grocery stores; gow gee, egg or spring roll pastry sheets can be substituted.

zucchini also known as courgette; small green or yellow vegetable belonging to the squash family.

INDEX

B
baked fish with sweet
  and sour sauce 114
baked garlic quail 32
barbecued chicken with
  chilli vinegar sauce 20
beef
  and mushroom salad 161
  char-grilled, salad 154
  chilli, with bamboo
    shoots 90
  crying tiger 13
  curry with onions and
    peanuts, dry 75
  curry with red and
    green chillies 72
  ginger, stir-fry 98
  massaman curry 71
  satay sticks, mixed 23
  salad, char-grilled 154
  soup, spicy 44
  steak, stir-fry, with
    green beans 89
  with noodles, crisp
    hot and sweet 93
  with oyster sauce 89

C
cabbage salad with lime
  juice dressing 169
cakes, fish 28
calamari salad 157
cauliflower, choy sum
  and snake beans,
    stir-fried 131
char-grilled beef salad 154
chiang mai noodles 146
chicken (see poultry)
chilli beef with bamboo
  shoots 90
chillies, red and green,
  with beef curry 72
choy sum, cauliflower
  and snake beans,
    stir-fried 131
cold prawn salad 157
coriander paste 27
crab fried rice in
  omelette 145
crab salad 161
crisp fish salad with
  chilli lime dressing 158
crisp fried noodles
  (mee krob) 142

crisp hot and sweet beef
  with noodles 93
crying tiger 31
cucumber dipping sauce 15
curry pastes
  curry (chilli beef with
    bamboo shoots) 90
  green 174
  massaman 71
  panang 175
  red 174
  yellow 175
curry
  beef massaman 71
  beef with red and
    green chillies 72
  chicken green 48
  chicken panang 67
  dry beef with onions
    and peanuts 75
  duck red 63
  fish and potato yellow 59
  fish ball and eggplant
    red 60
  pork and pickled
    garlic green 51
  pork jungle 55
  pork with eggplant 52
  puffs 19
  red chicken 64
  seafood and thai
    eggplant, yellow 56
  vegetables, green 68

D
dipping sauce, cucumber 15
dipping sauce, sweet chilli 19
dry beef curry with onions
  and peanuts 75
duck red curry 63
duck stir-fry, tamarind 81

E
egg and tofu salad 173
eggplant and fish ball
  red curry 60
eggplant tofu, stir-fried 127
eggplant with pork curry 52

F
fish (see seafood)

G
green beans with steak,
  stir-fried 89

green curry vegetables 68
green curry, chicken 48
green curry, pork and
  pickled garlic 51
green papaya salad 170

H
hot and sour fish steamed
  in banana leaves 106
hot and sweet beef, crisp,
  with noodles 93

L
lamb with basil and
  vegetables 102
larb tofu 123
larb, ginger and mint, with
  minced pork salad 162
lemon grass and lime
  fish parcels 114
lychee and pork salad 165

M
massaman curry, beef 71
minced pork salad with
  ginger and mint larb 162
mixed satay sticks 23
mixed seafood soup 40
mixed seafood with
  crisp thai basil 109
mixed vegetables in
  coconut milk 128
money bags 12
mushroom and beef
  salad 161
mussels with basil and
  lemon grass 110

N
noodles
  and chicken soup 44
  chiang mai 146
  crisp fried (mee krob) 142
  crisp hot and sweet
    beef with 93
  garlic pork with fried 150
  thai fried rice stick 134
  sweet soy fried
    (pad sieu/chicken) 141

O
octopus, stir-fried with
  thai basil 82
omelette, crab fried
  rice in 145

P
pad thai, vegetarian 124
palm sugar dressing 113
panang curry, chicken 67
papaya salad, green 170
paste, coriander 27
peanut sauce 131
pomelo salad 169
pork
  and lemon grass
    stir-fry 86
  and lychee salad 165
  and pickled garlic
    green curry 51
  curry with eggplant 52
  curry, jungle 55
  garlic, with fried
    noodles 150
  noodles, crisp fried
    (mee krob) 142
  salad with ginger and
    mint larb, minced 162
  satay sticks, mixed 23
  sticky, on broccolini 94
  sticky, with kaffir
    lime leaves 27
  thai fried rice stick
    noodles 134
  with eggplant 97
poultry
  chicken and galangal
    soup (tom ka gai) 43
  chicken and noodle
    soup 44
  chicken and thai basil
    fried rice 138
  chicken and thai basil
    stir-fry 78
  chicken, barbecued, with
    sweet vinegar sauce 20
  chicken, chilli and kaffir
    lime stir fry 82
  chicken green curry 48
  chiang mai noodles
    (chicken) 146
  chicken panang curry 67
  curry, red chicken 64
  duck red curry 63
  duck stir-fry, tamarind 81
  quail, baked garlic 32
  quail with fresh chilli
    and basil 32
  salad, spicy chicken 166
  satay sticks, mixed 23

sweet soy fried noodles
(pad sieu/chicken) 141
wings, deep-fried,
stuffed (chicken) 16
prawn(s)
balls, deep-fried 24
fried rice with 137
salad, cold 157
soup, spicy sour
(tom yum goong) 36
with garlic 85
puffs, curry 19
pumpkin, basil and chilli
stir-fry 120

Q

quail with fresh chilli
and basil 32
quail, baked garlic 32

R

red chicken curry 64
red curry, duck 63
red curry, fish ball
and eggplant 60
rice
black 149
chicken and thai basil
fried rice 138
crab fried rice in
omelette 145
fried, with prawns 137
glutinous 149
jasmine, steamed 149
yellow coconut 150

S

salad
apple, green, with
salmon cutlets 113
beef and mushroom 161
beef, char-grilled 154
cabbage with lime
juice dressing 169
calamari 157
chicken, spicy
(larb gai) 166
crab 161
fish with chilli lime
dressing, crisp 158
green papaya 170
pomelo 169
pork and lychee 165
pork with ginger and
mint larb, minced 162

prawn, cold 157
tofu and egg 173
tofu, spicy 173
sauces
chilli vinegar 20
crying tiger 31
cucumber dipping 15
peanut 131
satay 23
sweet and sour 114
sweet chilli 12
sweet chilli dipping 19
sweet chilli peanut 16
seafood
calamari salad 157
crab fried rice in
omelette 145
crab salad 161
fish and potato
yellow curry 59
fish ball and eggplant
red curry 60
fish cakes 28
fish in spicy coconut
cream 110
fish parcels, lemon grass
and lime 114
fish salad with chilli lime
dressing, crisp 158
fish steamed in banana
leaves, hot and
sour 106
fish, grilled, with sweet-
sour dressing 117
fish, baked, with sweet
and sour sauce 114
fish, steamed, with chilli
and ginger 117
mussels with basil
and lemon grass 110
noodles, crisp fried
(mee krob) 142
octopus, stir-fried, with
thai basil 82
prawn balls, deep-fried 24
prawns, fried rice with 137
prawn salad, cold 157
prawn soup, spicy sour
(tom yum goong) 36
prawns with garlic 85
salad, calamari 157
salad, cold prawn 157
salmon cutlets with green
apple salad 113

seafood and thai eggplant
yellow curry 56
seafood soup, mixed 40
seafood soup, spicy 39
seafood, mixed, with
crisp thai basil 109
seafood, stir-fried,
with basil 101
tom yum goong (spicy
sour prawn soup) 36
soup
spicy beef 44
chicken and galangal
(tom ka gai) 43
chicken and noodle 44
prawn, spicy sour
(tom yum goong) 36
seafood, mixed 40
seafood, spicy 39
spring rolls 15
steak with green beans,
stir-fried 89
steamed jasmine rice 149
stir fries
bamboo shoots with
chilli beef 90
beef, ginger 98
beef with oyster sauce 89
broccolini, sticky
pork on 94
cauliflower, choy sum
and snake beans 131
chicken and thai basil 78
chicken, chilli and
kaffir lime 82
chilli beef with bamboo
shoots 90
choy sum, cauliflower
and snake beans 131
duck, tamarind 81
eggplant tofu 127
eggplant with pork 97
ginger beef 98
lamb with basil and
vegetables 102
octopus with thai basil 82
pork and lemon grass 86
pork on broccolini,
sticky 94
prawns with garlic 85
pumpkin, basil and
chilli 120
seafood with basil 101
steak with green beans 89

sticky pork on
broccolini 94
vegetables with cracked
black pepper 102
vegetables, sweet
and sour 94

T

tamarind duck stir-fry 81
thai fried rice stick noodles
(pad thai) 134
tofu
and egg salad 173
deep-fried, with
peanut sauce 131
larb 123
spicy, salad 173
stir-fried eggplant 127

V

vegetables
and lamb with basil 102
green curry 68
in coconut milk,
mixed 128
stir-fried sweet
and sour 94
stir-fried with cracked
black pepper 102
vegetarian pad thai 124
vegetarian
black rice 149
cauliflower, choy sum
and snake beans,
stir-fried 131
eggplant tofu,
stir-fried 127
glutinous rice 149
green curry vegetables 68
jasmine rice,
steamed 149
larb tofu 123
pomelo salad 169
pumpkin, basil and
chilli stir-fry 120
seafood and thai eggplant
yellow curry 56
tofu, deep-fried, with
peanut sauce 131
tofu, larb 123
tofu and egg salad 173
vegetables in coconut
milk, mixed 128
vegetarian pad thai 124
yellow coconut rice 150

CONVERSION CHART

measures

One Australian metric measuring cup holds approximately 250ml, one Australian metric tablespoon holds 20ml, one Australian metric teaspoon holds 5ml.

The difference between one country's measuring cups and another's is within a two- or three-teaspoon variance, and will not affect your cooking results. North America, New Zealand and the United Kingdom use a 15ml tablespoon.

All cup and spoon measurements are level. The most accurate way of measuring dry ingredients is to weigh them. When measuring liquids, use a clear glass or plastic jug with the metric markings.

We use large eggs with an average weight of 60g.

dry measures

metric	imperial
15g	½oz
30g	1oz
60g	2oz
90g	3oz
125g	4oz (¼lb)
155g	5oz
185g	6oz
220g	7oz
250g	8oz (½lb)
280g	9oz
315g	10oz
345g	11oz
375g	12oz (¾lb)
410g	13oz
440g	14oz
470g	15oz
500g	16oz (1lb)
750g	24oz (1½lb)
1kg	32oz (2lb)

liquid measures

metric	imperial
30ml	1 fluid oz
60ml	2 fluid oz
100ml	3 fluid oz
125ml	4 fluid oz
150ml	5 fluid oz (¼ pint/1 gill)
190ml	6 fluid oz
250ml	8 fluid oz
300ml	10 fluid oz (½ pint)
500ml	16 fluid oz
600ml	20 fluid oz (1 pint)
1000ml (1 litre)	1¾ pints

length measures

metric	imperial
3mm	⅛in
6mm	¼in
1cm	½in
2cm	¾in
2.5cm	1in
5cm	2in
6cm	2½in
8cm	3in
10cm	4in
13cm	5in
15cm	6in
18cm	7in
20cm	8in
23cm	9in
25cm	10in
28cm	11in
30cm	12in (1ft)

oven temperatures

These oven temperatures are only a guide for conventional ovens. For fan-forced ovens, check the manufacturer's manual.

	°C (Celsius)	°F (Fahrenheit)	Gas Mark
Very slow	120	250	½
Slow	150	275-300	1-2
Moderately slow	170	325	3
Moderate	180	350-375	4-5
Moderately hot	200	400	6
Hot	220	425-450	7-8
Very hot	240	475	9